THE *Hillier* GARDENER'S GUIDES

Climbers & Wall Plants

Philippa Bensley

D&C
David and Charles

D0258621

A DAVID & CHARLES BOOK
Copyright © David & Charles Limited 2006

David & Charles is an F+W Publications Inc. company
4700 East Galbraith Road
Cincinnati, OH 45236

First published in the UK in 2006

Text copyright © Philippa Bensley 2006

Philippa Bensley has asserted her right to be identified as author of this
work in accordance with the Copyright, Designs and Patents Act, 1988.

All rights reserved. No part of this publication may be reproduced,
stored in a retrieval system, or transmitted, in any form or by any means,
electronic or mechanical, by photocopying, recording or otherwise,
without prior permission in writing from the publisher.

A catalogue record for this book is available from the British Library.

ISBN-13: 978-0-7153-2303-8
ISBN-10: 0-7153-2303-2

Printed in Singapore by KHL Printing Co Pte Ltd
for David & Charles
Brunel House   Newton Abbot   Devon

Produced for David & Charles by
OutHouse Publishing, Winchester, Hampshire SO22 5DS

Series Consultant Andrew McIndoe

For OutHouse Publishing:
Series Editor Sue Gordon
Art Editor Robin Whitecross
Editors Lesley Riley, Polly Boyd
Design Assistant Caroline Wollen
Proofreader Audrey Horne
Indexer June Wilkins

For David & Charles:
Commissioning Editor Mic Cady
Art Editor Sue Cleave
Designer Sarah Clark
Production Controller Beverley Richardson

Visit our website at www.davidandcharles.co.uk

David & Charles books are available from all good bookshops;
alternatively you can contact our Orderline on 0870 9908222
or write to us at FREEPOST EX2 110, D&C Direct, Newton Abbot,
TQ12 4ZZ (no stamp required UK only); US customers call
800-289-0963 and Canadian customers call 800-840-5220.

Previous page (left to right): *Actinidia kolomikta*, *Rosa* 'Zéphirine
Drouhin', *Clematis* 'Markham's Pink'.
Above (left to right): *Clematis macropetala* seedheads, *Clematis*
'Polish Spirit', *Hedera helix* 'Atropurpurea', *Parthenocissus
tricuspidata* 'Lowii', *Chaenomeles speciosa* 'Geisha Girl', *Clematis*
'Huldine'.

ORNAMENTAL PLANT OR PERNICIOUS WEED?

In certain circumstances ornamental garden plants
can be undesirable when introduced into natural
habitats, either because they compete with native flora,
or because they act as hosts to fungal and insect pests.
Plants that are popular in one part of the world may be
considered undesirable in another.
Horticulturists have learned to be wary of the effect that
cultivated plants may have on native habitats and,
as a rule, any plant likely to be a problem in a particular
area if it escapes from cultivation is restricted and
therefore is not offered for sale.

ESSEX COUNTY
COUNCIL LIBRARY

Contents

Introduction

Climbers have always been my favourite plants. My earliest childhood memories are coloured with them – the deliciously scented honeysuckle that wound its elegant way round the windows of the house, the solanum that hung over the garden swing seat, and the richly scented rambling rose that escaped over the wall from the plantswoman's garden next door.

Spending my teens in sheltered south Cornwall introduced me to the glamour of evergreen magnolias with their massive 'dinner plate' flowers. I also discovered my great passion – clematis. The soft shell-pink *Clematis* 'Hagley Hybrid', the big bold iridescent flowers of *Clematis* 'Nelly Moser' and the enchanting double flowers of *Clematis* 'Proteus' all made a huge impression on me at this time. They also led me to the exciting catalogue of the great Jim Fisk who, in the 1970s, was just rekindling the public passion for clematis at the Chelsea Flower Show, and to Christopher Lloyd's book *Clematis*, filled with his dry humour and wise words.

Now, many years later, as plant buyer and adviser for Hillier Garden Centres, I am lucky enough to see wonderful new climbers going from first discovery to public launch – with me on the other side of the rope at the Chelsea Flower Show this time.

This book is based on the questions I am asked daily at Hillier. It is divided into different sections to enable you to find answers easily, and gives tips on how to use climbers and how to get the best from them by avoiding planting pitfalls and by appropriate pruning and training. It also provides a choice of plants for particular situations, advises on the use of colour and discusses climbers through the seasons. Lots of suggestions for wonderful planting combinations appear throughout.

The book looks at a wide range of plants while taking into account the popular appeal of the big four climbers – clematis, roses, honeysuckles and ivies. It will also act as your personal plant adviser, telling you when a plant is worth its weight in gold and when it is not!

I hope this book answers all the questions you may have hesitated to ask at the garden centre and encourages you to be adventurous and try some new plants. Climbers are fantastic value and one of the key elements in a successful garden.

Philippa Bensley

WHAT IS A CLIMBER?

The botanical definition of a climber is straightforward: a climber is a plant that has developed adaptations to enable it to climb, such as tendrils, stem roots, self-clinging pads or long, flexible stems. However, gardeners tend to apply the term much more broadly, to include any plant used to cover a wall, a fence or any other kind of structure.

So, with this in mind, we cannot consider a book on climbers without including wall shrubs. Many shrubs – woody plants that have more than one stem arising from ground level – are seen much more often growing against a wall than in open ground; ceanothus, pyracantha and chaenomeles are all favourites.

Both annual and perennial climbers are included in this book. Annuals, for example sweet pea (*Lathyrus odoratus*), complete their life cycle in a year; perennials, such as clematis, live for three years or more. Bear in mind that a plant's life span may vary according to the local climate.

Conservatory plants are also featured. Generally, these are exotic, tender climbers that need to be grown under cover, but some are superb outdoors in sheltered areas, even in colder regions. In warmer countries such plants are garden staples – for example, bougainvilleas.

The RHS Award of Garden Merit ♀

The Royal Horticultural Society (RHS) gives its Award of Garden Merit to plants that have a long season of interest, are easy to grow and are available through a reasonable number of nurseries or garden centres. The award is denoted by the symbol ♀, which appears immediately after the plant name on labels and in catalogues and other publications – including this one. For gardeners facing the bewildering range of plants available, it is a good guide to whether a particular variety is a worthwhile one to choose. This does not necessarily mean that a plant without the award is inferior: many new varieties have not yet been assessed and some excellent plants are not sufficiently widely available to qualify.

LEFT: *Clematis* 'Hagley Hybrid'.

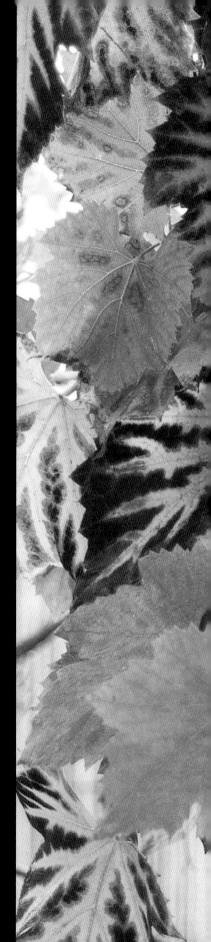

INTRODUCING CLIMBERS

Climbers are indispensable in gardens. From early times they have been valued by gardeners for their versatility, their flowers, their ornamental foliage and sometimes their fruit. They lengthen the period of interest, highlight focal points and mask less attractive features. With planning they will adorn other plants in their quieter seasons and cover surfaces, both vertical and horizontal, with a cloak of flowers and foliage. Climbers are easy to grow; they are rarely greedy on space and, to the delight of the gardener, most grow and perform quickly.

RIGHT: *Vitis* 'Brant'

A history of climbing plants

Valued initially as little more than a source of food and drink, climbers started to come into their own when grown to provide shade and privacy. Later, as man – and plants – travelled the world, botanists and breeders were quick to appreciate the versatility and ornamental qualities of climbers.

Native climbers are few and far between, and many – for example, the British *Clematis vitalba* (traveller's joy or old man's beard) – may be charming additions to our hedgerows but are hardly spectacular garden plants. When man first began to cultivate plants, there was little to inspire him to decorate his plot and his primary concern was to provide food for himself.

EARLY GARDENS

The Romans, like many others, adapted Egyptian gardening ideals of formality and discipline to suit their lives and when they arrived in Britain they brought these ideals with them, introducing gardening as part of civilized life. They imported many flowering plants acquired from across the empire. They also introduced grape vines, partly in the hopes that they might wean the locals from their love of ale, which they brewed from the native hop, *Humulus lupulus*. The climate was milder then than it is now, and the grape vines thrived in vineyards throughout southern England. The rare property of retaining its leaves through the winter led to *Hedera helix*, the English ivy, being highly valued by pagans and Christians alike. The Romans thought it a symbol of great learning and frequently used it in garlands and wreaths.

Following the fall of the Roman empire, the Dark Ages are often seen as a particularly low spot in gardening history, but in fact the garden was alive and thriving, carefully nurtured by monks, who found sensual as well as physical refreshment in their gardens. The monastic walled gardens were often built round a well and housed a collection of mainly medicinal and culinary plants. The inclusion of arbours in many monastery gardens points to the awareness, at the very least, of a contemplative purpose to gardens.

The grape vine, *Vitis vinifera*, is part of the lasting legacy of the Roman era, during which time it thrived in southern England.

The Norman invasion of Britain saw the birth of the country's great castles. Stark and workmanlike, they were fighting fortresses, and their lords had no time for frivolities such as gardening. However, the introduction of a strict code of chivalry was to lead to the birth of the English knight and thus, unwittingly, were sown the seeds of the modern garden. For these knights joined the Crusades and travelled to the Middle East and Spain, where they were dazzled by the Moors' sumptuous walled gardens. These were a refuge from the outside world, calm oases full of exotic plant material. Water spilled from fountains and watercourses, and pergolas created shaded walkways for the ladies. These same knights eventually returned to their grim fortified castles in Britain, bringing many sophisticated planting ideas and transforming their gardens, complete with arbours and pergolas, into perfect settings for the rituals of courtly love. As early as AD 1400 the first English gardening book, *The Feate of Gardening*, gave advice on growing many plants including 'Honysoke' (*Lonicera periclymenum*) and 'Vines' (*Vitis vinifera*). Contemporary illustrations show trellis with climbing roses and tunnel arbours covered with vines.

INTO THE RENAISSANCE

As life became more stable, the home no longer needed to serve as a fortress, and the manor house became the newest fashion. The south-facing front of the house featured pleasure gardens designed for 'delight and enjoyment': the climbing plant had begun to find its place.

The Tudors and Elizabethans loved scented plants and *Lonicera periclymenum* (the woodbine or common honeysuckle) moved from the hedgerow into the garden, along with the only British native climbing rose, *Rosa arvensis*. The willow bower, swathed in clouds of scented sweetbriar roses (*Rosa rubiginosa*) and honeysuckle, was the perfect venue for trysts and secret assignations.

The British began to build on their instinctive love of gardening. The peasant still had to concentrate on growing food to keep his family alive but decorative flowers found their way into all but the poorest of cottage gardens. The wealthy merchant classes, meanwhile, had time for the niceties of life, perhaps even time to play. Curiosity about the natural world took hold, and new books on botany found their way into print. Britain's first botanic garden was founded in Oxford in the early 1620s.

NEW WORLD, NEW PLANTS

The arrival of the Pilgrim Fathers in America in 1620 heralded a busy exchange of plants across the Atlantic. Plant collector John Tradescant the Elder visited Virginia, introducing to Britain the Virginia creeper (*Parthenocissus quinquefolia*), and his son took home the 'Indian honeysuckle' (*Lonicera sempervirens*), later planted by George Washington at Mount Vernon – and still growing

This hazel tunnel arbour in Queen Eleanor's Garden, Winchester, is planted with *Lonicera periclymenum* and *Rosa rubiginosa*. Both were grown for shade and scent in the time of Henry III's queen.

there. Both North and South America proved to be a rich source of new plant material for Britain.

Plant collecting gathered momentum over the 18th and 19th centuries as trading routes expanded, first in the South Seas, then in the Far East. By the mid-1800s Victorian botanists were being sponsored by their wealthy patrons to travel the world and bring back prized specimens of plants. Some of our best-loved climbers were sent home from China and the Far East by the plant hunter Robert Fortune in the mid-1800s. *Wisteria sinensis* (Chinese wisteria), *Lonicera japonica* (Japanese honeysuckle) and

The John Tradescants, father and son, visited America and took home many climbers still familiar today, for example *Parthenocissus quinquefolia* (left) and *Lonicera sempervirens* (above).

The influx of new plant material, including *Wisteria sinensis* (1), *Lonicera japonica* (2), *Jasminum officinale* (3), and a breeding craze that produced plants like *Clematis* 'Jackmanii' (4) and *Rosa* 'Albéric Barbier' (5) made gardening particularly fascinating in the 19th century.

Jasminum officinale (common jasmine) started to grace the walls of homes and gardens. Those that were too tender to withstand the weather found a place in the conservatory. Armed with this wealth of new material, plant breeders embarked on a frenzied programme of hybridization. One of our favourite climbers was a result of this. In 1862 George Jackman, a nurseryman in Woking, Surrey, crossed the largest-flowered of all clematis species, *Clematis lanuginosa*, which Fortune had discovered in 1851, with an existing hybrid and created the rich purple *Clematis* 'Jackmanii'. The sensation this caused prompted a flurry of breeding work and in just 50 years clematis went from a handful of species to more than 500 varieties.

Then, just as quickly as it started, this craze came to a dramatic end. A new disease caused the new hybrids to collapse and die within a matter of hours. Clematis wilt had arrived. This abrupt end to clematis breeding was undoubtedly to our benefit, since only those varieties with true strength in their breeding remain today.

The rose was also a beneficiary of this breeding boom. Rambling roses had been slipping into Europe since the 1700s but without causing much of a stir. However, the discovery of a crimson rose in a Tokyo garden by British engineer Robert Smith changed all that. He sent it home to a friend in Scotland and when exhibited in 1893 it caused such a sensation that Queen Victoria made a special trip to see it. The breeding activity that followed, in America as well as Europe, produced some of the most famous roses we know today, including *Rosa* 'Rambling Rector', 'Veilchenblau' and 'Albéric Barbier'.

INTO THE 20TH CENTURY

Other plants now regained breeders' attention and gardeners began to grow a far wider range of climbers. Garden design had become the province of the ordinary house-owner, and arbours and trellis were the order of the day. The pergola, in common use in Italy for centuries, became hugely popular and a trademark (together with the rill) of the Arts and Crafts style of garden. In the early part of the 20th century the partnership of British plantswoman Gertrude Jekyll and architect Edwin Lutyens did much to raise the profile of climbers, with Lutyens' stunning brick-built pergolas draped in aristolochias, vines and *Ampelopsis*, as well as wisteria, roses and clematis.

The Arts and Crafts movement favoured stone- and brick-built pergolas (left). New roses, such as *Rosa* 'New Dawn' (above), were perfect for clothing the uprights.

Gardeners with arbours, trellises and pergolas welcomed the wider availability of two forms of honeysuckle, *Lonicera periclymenum* 'Serotina' and *Lonicera periclymenum* 'Belgica', whose stems were more pliable than those of the species, allowing them to be contorted into an arbour of whatever shape was currently in vogue. Meanwhile, in 1910, Dr Van Fleet, an American hybridist, crossed *Rosa wichuriana* with a repeat flowering tea rose to produce a pretty, pale pink rose that was named after him. Nature intervened here and a sport appeared on one of his unsold plants left in the field. The sport, named *Rosa* 'New Dawn', proved a dramatic breakthrough – it was the first modern repeat-flowering climbing rose.

The changes in society brought about by the two world wars had a significant effect on the gardening world. Labour was scarce and the big aristocratic estates went into decline. After World War II, those seeking a career in horticulture looked to nurseries for employment, rather than big estates. It was through the nurseries that new plants were coming into the country, and many became the launch pad for modern plantsmen. The 1950s and 1960s saw gardening back on the scene in a big way.

Garden 'features' were in fashion again and we needed climbers to cover them. Jim Fisk led a resurgence of interest in clematis in the 1970s with his ground-breaking displays at the Chelsea Flower Show. Thanks to modern chemicals, the spectre of clematis wilt had receded and gardeners were as keen as ever to get hold of new plants. Fisk opened our eyes to the work of eastern European breeders and nowadays the work of breeders such as Uno and Aili Kivistik in Estonia is receiving particular acclaim, for example *Clematis* 'Rüütel', *Clematis* 'Viola' and *Clematis* 'Piilu'.

WHAT OF THE FUTURE?

At the start of the 21st century, gardens are becoming increasingly smaller and space has to be made to work much harder. Climbers fulfil many planting roles, not only adding a vital vertical dimension to gardens, but doubling as screens or ground cover and scrambling through trees and shrubs to provide an additional burst of colour.

The 1990s saw a concentration by breeders on the 'novelty' climber, but gardeners are now tiring of the rush for the latest new plant, and good garden plants are back in vogue. Luckily there is a huge bank, from the great plant-hunting days, of little-known material, whose possibilities are still to be explored. The quest for more compact varieties of existing plants such as roses and clematis also continues.

Nurseryman Fred Godfrey found this new, as yet un-named gold-leaved clematis.

11

Speaking botanically

Many gardeners are wary of botanical Latin and use common names instead, but botanical Latin is there to help. It gives every plant, and each variation of it, a distinct, unique name. Even better, this name is the same no matter what language you speak. Sometimes pronunciation may be the barrier to using 'proper' names. It shouldn't be: a room of so-called experts would be unable to agree between CLEM-a-tis or clem-A-tis, so why waste valuable time worrying about it?

FAMILY There are many families in the plant world, resembling something like flower tribes. Classification is based on the shape of the flowers. The family name is not in everyday use. All family names start with a capital letter and end in -aceae. For example, the rose family is called Rosaceae, while all clematis belong to the Ranunculaceae, or buttercup family.

GENUS A genus links together species that are closely related; the generic name is equivalent to our surname. The generic name always starts with a capital letter and is usually a noun. It is treated as Latin and as such has a gender. Often derived from Greek, Latin or Arabic, it may describe the plant or commemorate a person, perhaps a botanist or horticulturist. For example, *Ampelopsis* is from the Greek *ampelos* (vine) and *opsis* (appearance, or resemblance) meaning vine-like; *Lonicera* is named after Adam Lonitzer a 16th-century German naturalist.

SPECIES The species name is like our first name, although it always appears after the generic name. It identifies a group of plants occurring in the wild with very similar characteristics. The species name is written in lower-case letters and the ending will change according to the gender of the genus name, as in *Camellia japonica*.

SPECIES NAMES FALL INTO FOUR MAIN CATEGORIES:

Describing origin: by continent or country, e.g. *japonicus, -a, -um,* from Japan.

Describing habitat: from mountains, woods, fields, water, e.g. *montanus, -a, -um,* of the mountains.

Describing the plant or a feature of it: such as shape, flower, leaf, colour, e.g. *macropetala,* large-petalled.

Commemorating a person: such as a plant hunter, botanist, patron or famous horticulturist, e.g. × *williamsii,* after J.C. Williams, the Cornish camellia hybridist.

SUBSPECIES, FORM OR VARIETY These are distinct variations occurring naturally in the wild species, for example colour or flower shape. They rank in the order they are given here and are denoted by the abbreviations subsp., f. and var. They are written in lower case. For example, *Hydrangea anomala* subsp. *petiolaris, Jasminum officinale* f. *affine* and *Parthenocissus himalayana* var. *rubrifolia.* The terms variety and form are also used more informally to refer to cultivars.

CULTIVAR The term cultivar is used for a variation of a plant that is not distinct enough to merit one of the titles above. A cultivar generally tends to be man-made through hybridization. It could also be a form collected from the wild that would die out if

SELLING NAMES

Many plants today are sold under a selling name, also known as a trade designation. This is different from the cultivar name and can also be a registered trademark. Usually a plant has only one selling name, but it can have several. The selling name is always shown in a different typeface, often in capital letters, and is followed by the cultivar name. For example, *Sophora* SUN KING ('Hilsop') and *Jasminum officinale* FIONA SUNRISE ('Frojas'). The cultivar name ensures that you do not mistakenly duplicate a purchase. Any translation of a foreign-language cultivar name is also treated as a selling name but in this case appears after the cultivar name. For example, *Clematis* 'Blekitny Aniol' (BLUE ANGEL).

PLANT BREEDERS' RIGHTS (PBR)

Certain plants may not be propagated for sale without royalties being paid to the registered breeder. Wherever such plants are offered for sale, the letters PBR must follow the plant name.

cross is given a new species name with an × before it, for example *Lonicera × tellmanniana* and *Chaenomeles × superba*. If the cross is too complicated, or a hybrid's parents are unknown, the new cultivar name is given directly after the genus, as in *Passiflora* 'Amethyst' and *Pyracantha* 'Orange Charmer'. A cross between genera is shown as an × before the new genus name. For example, × *Fatshedera* is a hybrid between *Fatsia* and *Hedera*.

NAME CHANGES

From time to time new evidence is produced that shows that, for a variety of reasons, a plant has been incorrectly named. This evidence may be overwhelming, in which case the name is changed immediately. At other times a proposed name change may be more controversial and further research will need to be undertaken. DNA testing may reveal unseen relationships involving renaming many plants – but that is something for the future. Old names, when they are well known, are often shown in parentheses after the new name. For example, *Clematis terniflora* (*Clematis paniculata*) and *Cotoneaster atropurpureus* 'Variegatus' (*Cotoneaster horizontalis* 'Variegatus').

left to fend for itself. The cultivar name is written with a capital letter and in single quotation marks. For example, *Clematis* 'Freda' and *Lonicera periclymenum* 'Sweet Sue'. Any offspring of a cultivar should be clones of the original plant – vegetatively propagated by cuttings or grafting and so identical in every way.

HYBRID A hybrid is a cross between two plants. Usually this is a cross between species of the same genus, but it can occasionally be between genera. A straightforward species

PLANT NAMES ARE FUN

Over time, many gardeners find they absorb hundreds of plant names. Understanding the meaning of these will open up a whole world of extra information about each plant. These are a few examples of descriptions used in the names of climbing plants:

SPECIES NAME	MEANING	EXAMPLE
caprifolium	(goat-leaved) climbing like a goat	*Lonicera caprifolium* (right)
complexa	complex, with interwoven branches	*Muehlenbeckia complexa*
lupulus	(wolf) with wolf's teeth, for climbing	*Humulus lupulus*
peregrinum	wandering, straggling in growth	*Tropaeolum peregrinum*
periclymenum	ancient Greek for honeysuckle	*Lonicera periclymenum*
radicans	creeping and rooting	*Campsis radicans*
scandens	climbing	*Cobaea scandens*
viticella	vine bower	*Clematis viticella*
volubilis	twisting round	*Aconitum volubile*

How to use climbers

Climbers fit really well into today's gardens. Far more than just coverings for walls and fences, they also make invaluable ground cover and quick-growing screens and can thread extra colour through shrubs, trees and other climbers. Be adventurous in how you use them, experimenting with swags, topiary and tunnels of flowers and foliage. Apply a basic understanding of how to put colours together and you can create planting schemes that are both beautiful and imaginative.

All climbing and rambling roses need to be tied in regularly to whatever support they are given.

LAYERED PLANTING

Garden designers talk a great deal about 'layered planting', meaning planting at different levels to maximize three-dimensional interest. The first 'layer' of colour is created by low planting such as perennials, bulbs, bedding and low-growing shrubs. The second layer consists of larger shrubs, and the third layer is composed of trees. Climbers are interesting in that they fit into all three layers. They can be used as ground cover, working well in most situations from dry shade to full sun. They contribute to the second layer when grown against walls and fences or when trained on obelisks and tripods, bringing a vital vertical element to borders – and doing this far more quickly than would trees or tall shrubs. Most importantly, though, they play a large part in the third layer. Although we think of trees as the prime choice for this third layer, in fact their appeal is fairly limited. Summer-flowering trees are very few and far between, and you have to rely on foliage colour for effect. However, rich rambling roses and jewel-coloured clematis draped elegantly through trees create stunning summer focal points and enhance the overall picture. In all three layers, growing climbers through other plants gives an extra dimension to the planting, bringing fresh colour to a tree or shrub either before its own flowers have bloomed or once they have finished.

GROWING CLIMBERS THROUGH OTHER CLIMBERS

The idea of planting climbers together to grow through one another may seem revolutionary, but it is how many grow in the wild. Clever combinations of climbers, whether on walls or fences or on structures such as pergolas and obelisks, can make a space seem larger. Choose plants either to flower at the same time for spectacular colour, or at different times to extend the season of interest.

Roses make lovely hosts for other climbers, the many forms of clematis offering a wide range to choose from. An evergreen plant, perhaps one with variegated foliage, could provide long-term interest, enhanced by a spring- or summer-flowering partner, or by another foliage climber with spectacular autumn colour.

Aesthetically, you will need to think about combinations of flower shape and size, as well as colour; the same applies to foliage, too. On the practical side, it is important to match partners for vigour, so that one does not completely swamp the other, and you also need to make sure the two enjoy the same growing conditions.

It is useful to recognize different tones of the same colour. These are, from the top left clockwise, blue red, yellow red, yellow pink and blue pink.

WALL SHRUBS

Wall shrubs are simply normal shrubs chosen to grow against a wall. They split into two groups. The first, and larger one, consists of those that need the warmth and support of a wall to bring out the best in them. In many cases this is because they are tender, and would not survive in the open garden, but it may also be because they appreciate shelter from wind, sun or rain. The smaller group is of those that look better against a wall, either because of its strong architectural presence or because they display their flowers or fruit better when trained in this way.

Most wall shrubs need tying to a support to a greater or lesser degree, depending on the level of formality you desire, but a few just like to grow next to, rather than against, a wall and resent being tied in.

Like many other wall shrubs, chaenomeles tend to show their flowers far better against a wall than when they are grown in open ground.

CLASSIC WALL SHRUBS

Abutilon, Camellia, Carpenteria, Ceanothus, Chaenomeles, Clianthus, Fremontodendron, Magnolia, Pyracantha

UNDERSTANDING COLOUR

Choosing colours that work together needs some understanding of their basic qualities. Although people often refer to hot and cool colours, this is misleading since it implies that cool colours are always cold in appearance, and nothing could be further from the truth.

A better way of classifying colours is to divide them into those that contain a dominant proportion of yellow and those that have blue as the dominant tone. All colours can be in either group depending on their make-up. Tomato and scarlet, for example, are yellow reds, while crimson and plum are blue reds.

Unlike colour in our homes, flower colour is very rarely seen in isolation, devoid of any foil. We may be planting a bright magenta rose, but it will be set against a background of forgiving green foliage. This is what enables us to use some rather strident colour combinations, which might otherwise be less successful.

PUTTING COLOURS TOGETHER

White, although not strictly a colour, is considered one for plant purposes. It goes with almost anything – except perhaps with orange and red, which are just too different from white. All other colours, whether pale pastels or dark rich shades, work with white.

COLOUR THEORY

When you begin to choose plants and are not sure which colours work together, visit your local art shop and invest in a colour wheel. The colours are arranged in segments on a circle, so their relationship can easily be seen.

Useful starting points for plant combinations are two colours next to one another on the wheel, such as yellow and lime green (left), two colours opposite one another, such as orange and blue (below left), or three colours equally spaced on the wheel, such as violet, green and orange (below).

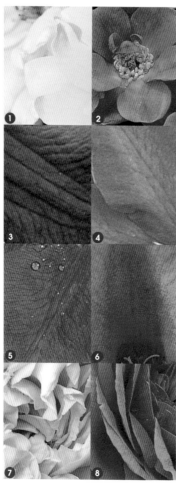

Yellow (1) works well with all the blues and purples. It also looks very vibrant with rich oranges and yellow-toned reds (2), but is not effective with blue-toned reds. It is also best avoided with pinks, whether yellow- or blue-based, unless you are feeling brave.

Red blends really well with all the bolder darker shades, although red and blue together is tiring for the eye so is not a combination to use if you want a restful result. Many of the 'black' shades fit into red because they are in fact a very dark plum (3). These need lighter colours to lift them otherwise they lose vibrancy. Blues (4) and oranges are good with deep plum.

Blue works with all colours and is good for making a transition between two 'difficult' colours such as pink and yellow in the garden. Unfortunately blue is the colour lacking in climbers, although the wide range of clematis in shades close to true blue does help to redress the balance. Purple (5) is also

a fantastic mixer: it works with every colour, whether yellow- or blue-based. As with the deep reds and blues, the deeper shades and purple-toned 'blacks' need some care to make sure that they do not disappear. Deep vibrant pinks (6) are wonderful with purple.

Orange ranges from pure citrus shades to the point where it blends with pink, a derivative of red, to make soft pinky tones such as salmon and peach (7). The clear shades are easy to use and fit in anywhere except with white. They can be combined with pink, but great skill is needed to get the colours just right.

Pink is the colour that causes the most problems; we tend to forget that it is in fact red with white added. Pinks with a pale blue tint (8) blend easily with all the other blue-tinted shades. These are the pastel pinks, blues and lavenders that appeal to so many gardeners. The yellow-toned pinks are much harder to use and need careful placing with deeper blues, purples and yellow-toned reds.

USING CLIMBERS CREATIVELY

Covering walls and fences and decorating arches and obelisks are perhaps our favourite ways of growing climbers, but these versatile plants lend themselves to any number of other creative uses. Consider the following ideas, but also let your imagination run wild and you are sure to come up with more.

SWAGS These are made by training climbers along thick rope, strung between large wooden uprights. They are a marvellous way of allowing rambling roses to show off their abundant blooms and the larger-growing clematis will also love winding their way along them. Green oak is an economic wood to use for the tall uprights; it will twist and crack with age but this adds to its character. The rope is threaded through holes drilled at the top of each post and must be secured with a knot on each side. Rope should be of a marine grade, otherwise it will quickly rot.

EDGING Climbers can make wonderful floral or foliage edging. Trained on a very low post-and-rail fence, regularly clipped ivy provides an elegant formal edging, while flowering climbers such as roses and sweet peas create a stunning informal effect. Regular tying in is essential to avoid the growth swarming over the path or border. Fruit trees, such as apple, trained as 'step-over' plants (that is, with a short, upright stem that then divides into two horizontal branches) also look very attractive lining a path.

TUNNELS Monet's garden at Giverny in France has the most wonderful wide rose arches spanning the long, broad path leading from the house. The vibrant ramblers reaching across to meet in the middle create a glorious tunnel effect when fully grown. This can be adapted for much smaller gardens using a run of round-topped arches or ready-made tunnel hoops. Clever planting at the base of the tunnel will ensure that it is not dull when out of flower. Large, bold tulips add colour in spring and take the eye lower, while a flowering shrub or other

Chains are an alternative to rope when making swags. *Clematis* ROSEMOOR is an ideal choice for covering the chains.

climber at the end of the tunnel can lead the eye through when flowering is over.

TOPIARY Creating topiary can be a slow business, but climbers allow you to cheat and have a fully formed topiary shape in a fraction of the time. *Hedera helix* (English ivy) and the tender *Ficus pumila* (climbing fig), both with neat, fairly small, evergreen foliage, are the best choices. You can either buy a topiary frame or make up your own from chicken wire. Packing it full of moist moss gives the climber something to root into, making it more likely to succeed.

CASCADES Climbing plants are most commonly seen growing up walls but in fact they climb down them rather more easily. More and more gardens now are built on steeply sloping ground, involving the use of retaining walls. Instead of trying to establish trailing plants at the top of such a wall, let climbers cascade over the edge. If you have plenty of room, lax-growing plants, for instance *Ceanothus* 'Yankee Point' or *Cotoneaster horizontalis,* are extremely effective. Where space is more limited, soft-stemmed climbers such as *Passiflora caerulea* and *Clematis montana* create stunning sheets of flower.

Buying climbers

The choice of climbers on display at a plant nursery or garden centre can be bewildering. Climbing plants are available in any size from a seedling to a mature specimen in a 200-litre container. So what do you need to know to help you make a selection?

When buying clematis choose the plant with the most stems at or near soil level, rather than the tallest plant.

YOUNG PLANTS

Seedlings and young plants in pots up to 1 litre in size are becoming more widely available because of the demand for cheaper plants.

Annual climbers are sold as seedlings or 'plug' plants early in the season. As the majority of these are grown by specialist nurseries, this is generally a reliable way of buying plants.

Perennial climbers are available in 9cm to 1-litre sizes, but can be more variable in quality. In reality, these sizes are suitable only for the enthusiast with facilities to grow plants on until they are big enough to be able to fend for themselves in the garden. This means a wait, usually of a year, before planting: not ideal for the average gardener.

FORMS OF SUPPORT

Climbers are traditionally sold with the stem tied to a single cane for support. The latest thinking suggests that a three-cane wigwam is better for young climbers. It provides more support than a single cane, stopping the stem from slipping down and cracking. This is especially important with clematis varieties susceptible to clematis wilt (see page 63), since a crack in the stem offers an ideal entry site for the infection.

Some plants are sold with a plastic net around the pot and cane. This is a poor system: removing the plant from the pot involves cutting through the net, often either breaking or twisting the stems in the process. You may be left with an unsightly plastic net on the plant: as the plant ages, this may eventually cut into the stems and allow disease to enter.

MAINSTREAM SIZES

The huge majority of climbers are grown in a 2- or 3-litre 'long tom' pot. This is a taller, narrower pot than usual, which suits the root structure of most climbers.

MEDIUM SIZES

Pots of 4–7.5 litres are usually reserved for those plants that are very vigorous. Greedy feeders such as roses, wisteria and campsis are good in this size of pot, tending to establish more quickly once planted. This size will be more expensive but the improved growth and flowering in the first few years make the extra money well spent.

WHAT TO LOOK FOR

When searching for a climber to suit a particular situation, it is best to visit a local nursery or garden centre, which will usually have a knowledgeable member of staff happy to offer advice. Whichever climber you choose, it must be healthy. Generally speaking, you are looking for:

- No weeds in the pot.
- No sign of pests or diseases.
- No roots coming from the bottom of the pot.
- More than one stem at the base of the plant.
- Evenly coloured foliage.

In terms of quality, often instinct is your best guide: if you feel unhappy about a plant then look elsewhere.

BUYING BARE-ROOT PLANTS

Most climbers and wall shrubs today are sold growing in containers and are available at any time of year. Roses, however, are often available as bare-root plants, dug up from the ground with no soil on the roots. Bare-root plants are generally cheaper than container-grown ones, but they are available for only a limited time each year – between mid-autumn and late winter, when they are dormant – and you can't see the plant's habit or true flower colour.

Bare-root climbers are commonly sold through mail order: always choose a well-known company and be sure to check the size or age of the plants you receive. Roses should be at least two years old. When they arrive, plant them straight away, or as soon as the ground is warm enough to dig.

SPECIMEN SIZES

Larger specimen plants – in pots from 10 to 200 litres – are increasingly available. You are buying time with a plant like this. The benefits are that the plant is much bigger initially – this may be important if you are trying to screen something quickly. The plant may also be in full flower when you buy it, which means you can see exactly what you are getting. Such plants are often already trained on a fan of trellis, and so look good in the garden from the outset. Specimen-size plants are also invaluable in a new garden: they can give an instant feeling of maturity. Evergreen climbers are often better value bought at specimen size because they usually grow more slowly than deciduous ones and so the time gained is greater.

The disadvantages are that larger plants are, of course, more expensive than young plants and large plants grown in containers need lots of water and protection from the elements. Once planted out, they tend not to receive that extra care and so many suffer a check in growth while they become established in their new, harsher environment. A smaller plant planted at the same time often catches up completely within a couple of years.

GROWING YOUR OWN NEW PLANTS

Taking softwood cuttings (that is, cuttings from young unripened stems) is an easy way to ensure that you always have new plants ready to replace short-lived wall shrubs. Take 7.5cm (3in) long lengths of stem early in the growing season and root them in pots of a proprietary cutting compost or an equal mix of peat or peat alternative and coarse grit. A 9cm pot will house several cuttings round the edge. Trim the cuttings just below a leaf joint and remove most of the leaves. Protect from strong sunlight. The time taken to root can be anything from two weeks upwards, depending on the genus.

Layering can be done at any time of the year and to all perennial climbers, although those with pliable stems such as honeysuckle (*Lonicera*) are easier to bring down to ground level. To layer a climber, take a stem and bend it down to the ground. Make an angled cut on the underside, almost, but not completely, severing the stem. Bury the stem in the ground, keeping the cut open, and hold it down with a metal pin or place a large stone on top of the soil. Once the layer has rooted and is producing new growth, cut the stem linking it to the parent plant.

How climbers climb

Climbing plants use a variety of methods to get themselves skywards. Some use aerial roots or suction pads to cling to a support; some twine themselves around it; and some – especially the rose – use thorns to get a good grip. Knowing how a climber will scale a wall or other structure and what help, if any, it will need saves costly mistakes.

SELF-SUPPORTING CLIMBERS

There are two groups of self-supporters – those with aerial roots and those with suction pads. After planting, both need a little temporary help to get a steady foothold because their grip develops as they grow. Using specially designed nails with lead tongues means that you can position each stem exactly where you want it and hold it still so that it gets off to a sure start.

Aerial roots appear on the stems of plants and fix themselves firmly to any suitable surface. The best-known climber with aerial roots is ivy (*Hedera*). It has a bad reputation as a wall wrecker but this is quite unjustified. Planting ivy on a sound wall with mortar in good condition will do no harm.

Of the group that uses suction pads, *Parthenocissus*, commonly called Virginia creeper, is the classic representative. It sends out tendrils from the stems, with little suction pads on the ends. These provide a cushioned coverage that helps the plant resist wind damage.

Self-supporting climbers are the obvious choice for really big cover-up jobs. Often they are large, boisterous plants and will happily romp up an ugly wall, or one where access is difficult, with minimal assistance.

In the wild, roses use their thorny stems to scramble through other plants; in order to climb a wall, they need tying to a support of a suitable height.

SOCIAL CLIMBERS

This group needs some help to reach their potential. Find out how big your climber gets so that you can be sure to give it a high enough support. So often a vigorous climber is seen valiantly trying to climb up the front of a house with the help of one tiny piece of trellis – a recipe for disappointment.

A number of plants climb by means of twining leaf-stalks, and of these clematis are the best known. The leaf-stalks are constantly feeling for any possible support; when they touch anything they mould themselves to its shape, allowing the new growth to forge on upwards. Climbers in this group make excellent companion plants since they do no damage to their hosts. These twining stalks are fairly persistent and continue providing support into winter, even after the leaves themselves have fallen.

Some plants use twining tendrils that grow from the stems of the plant and actively seek support. Passion flower (*Passiflora*) is the best-known representative. These tendrils support the plant over a number of seasons, even on deciduous climbers, because they are independent of the leaves. Plants in this group often twine around their own stems, creating a very strong structure that almost becomes self-supporting.

Climbers with twining stems send up long new growths that seek out a support and then wind their stems around it. Most plants wind in a clockwise direction but a few break this rule and wind anti-clockwise. This is a useful way of telling *Wisteria sinensis* (Chinese wisteria) from *Wisteria floribunda* (Japanese wisteria) – the Chinese species winds clockwise, and the Japanese anti-clockwise.

Roses and some bougainvilleas are more basic in their methods, relying on their thorns to hoist themselves up through other plants. Rambler roses are best adapted for climbing in this way, being closest to wild species and frequently having thorns that turn backwards to give the best grip.

If you have a garden feature such as an arbour or pergola to cover, then social climbers are your best choices. House walls and garden fences are also good homes, while trees, large shrubs and other climbers provide natural supports.

SELF-SUPPORTERS

AERIAL ROOTS

Campsis

Euonymus

Hedera (1)

Hydrangea anomala subsp. *petiolaris*

Pileostegia

Schizophragma

SUCTION PADS

Parthenocissus (2)

SOCIAL CLIMBERS

TWINING LEAF-STALKS

Clematis (3)

Lathyrus

TWINING TENDRILS

Ampelopsis

Passiflora

Vitis (4)

TWINING STEMS

Actinidia

Akebia

Fallopia

Humulus

Jasminum (some are shrubby)

Lonicera

Trachelospermum

Wisteria (5)

THORNS

Bougainvillea

Rosa (6)

Growing conditions

Climbers may be the choicest plants in a garden, yet their life can be far from easy. Knowing the conditions of the site you have in mind and choosing plants to suit your garden's soil type, aspect and microclimates can make a huge difference to their chances of success.

Vines (*Vitis*) prefer a neutral to alkaline soil with plenty of humus; the addition of well-rotted compost increases humus without making it more acidic.

WHAT IS A FROST POCKET?

Frost is a layer of cold air that flows like water across the land and, just like water, settles where it gets trapped. When gardeners have two identical plants growing close to one another and one thrives while the other struggles, the cause is often a frost pocket holding the harmful air around one of them. There is very little you can do about a frost pocket unless it is caused by a man-made feature, such as a hedge on the side or at the foot of a hill; if there is a gate in the hedge, leaving it open allows the frost to flow on through it.

Take a close look at the site before deciding which plant to buy. We all know the basics of warm, sheltered aspects and cold, exposed ones, but what else is there to consider? First take a look at the lie of the land. If the proposed planting site is in a dip or hollow or at the bottom of a hill, it may well be a frost pocket, a cold spot that is unsuitable for all but the toughest plants.

TYPES OF SOIL

It is important to identify your garden's soil type. All soils consist of varying proportions of minerals (particles of rock more or less broken down) and organic matter (decayed remains of living organisms). The soil structure will govern how well it drains and how well it retains nutrients. Coarse, sandy soils will be quick to absorb warmth, easy to dig and free-draining, but they are also low in nutrients and suffer from drought in dry weather. A fine clay soil will be almost the exact opposite, but it too will suffer in dry weather, baking hard in the sun.

The acidity or alkalinity of the soil (its pH) will also govern your choice of plants to some extent: while most plants prefer a neutral to slightly acid soil, ericaceous or acid-loving plants, for example, really must have an acid soil and will not thrive in an alkaline one. You cannot always tell the pH of your soil from its appearance; while pieces of chalk and flint generally indicate an alkaline soil, some soils, such as clay, can be either acid or alkaline. For a rough guide, look at what is thriving in gardens around you: blue hydrangeas indicate an acid soil, while pink ones indicate alkaline soil. Testing kits are available that will give you a much more accurate picture.

PLANTING TIME

Your soil type will greatly influence the time of planting. While container-grown plants can be planted at any season, there are still times of the year when planting is most successful.

With warm, sandy soils that can easily be dug all year, it is best not to plant in the height of summer: such soils hold very little moisture and plants will need plenty of extra watering. The same is true of chalk soil.

Where the soil is heavy clay, planting is also best avoided in really hot summers, since clay tends to dry out into a solid mass and crack badly. Deepest winter, when it is very cold and wet, is not a good planting time either. On clay, late summer and autumn and early spring planting are best.

Like all roses, *Rosa* 'American Pillar' revels in clay soils because they store large quantities of nutrients.

Improving any of these soils would allow a wider window for planting. Owners of a fertile, moisture-retentive loam are able to plant all year round.

IMPROVING YOUR SOIL

The single biggest tool you have at your disposal for growing superb climbers, no matter what your soil type, is soil improvement, essentially working towards a more crumbly, open texture that drains freely and retains plenty of nutrients.

To retain moisture and nutrients on sandy and chalk soils, work in plenty of ground or composted bark, well-rotted manure or garden compost, or leaf mould. The same materials will also improve drainage on clay soil, and you can also use coarse grit, gravel or horticultural sand.

There are climbers for every soil extreme. Fremontodendrons (left) love a chalky, alkaline soil, while camellias (right) detest it and need acid soil.

Practical planting

Thoughtful planting is the secret of successful climbers. Put as much effort into preparing the site as you do into choosing the plant. Thinking about the practicalities of the designated planting spot in advance, choosing supports with care, and understanding what to do when planting will bring the best results.

PROVIDING SUPPORTS

Choosing the right support for your climber is vitally important. First find out how big and heavy your chosen plant gets; vigorous climbers such as *Fallopia baldschuanica* (Russian vine or mile-a-minute) will fell a wooden fence quite easily, as can *Clematis montana*. The shrubby climbers *Jasminum officinale* and *Solanum crispum* 'Glasnevin' are very bushy and will extend a good 2m (6ft) either side of any support. Make sure your neighbour will appreciate their company. If not, plant them against a solid structure so that their growth stays in your garden.

SUPPORTS FOR WALLS When deciding on a method of support, aim to choose one in keeping with its setting. Modern architecture demands a look with simple,

Installing supports before planting (above) ensures that climbers, such as this *Rosa* 'Constance Spry' (right), cover a whole area. Long, screw-in vine-eyes make sure that air is able to circulate behind fully grown cliimbers.

PAINTING WALLS AND FENCES

Paint walls and treat fences or any other support before planting and the climbers will actually protect the finish. Deciduous climbers will allow some keyhole painting in the dormant season, but be careful not to get paint on the stems. The same applies to wood preservatives: many are harmful and need to be used with extreme caution near plant material.

uncluttered lines, while a more traditional approach is appropriate for period buildings. Trellis is usually the first candidate considered (see box, below). It can be extremely successful, but it requires a huge effort to fix it any higher than head height. If you are using trellis then you must cover the whole area that you intend to clothe before planting. Don't deceive yourself into thinking that you will cover the upper storey of the house when the plant eventually reaches it – you won't.

Trellis is often fixed directly to walls. This is not correct. You must put wooden blocks behind the trellis to create an air space of at least 10cm (4in).

Using wires stretched between vine-eyes screwed into the wall is often the best solution. This kind of support is extremely flexible, easily following the contours of any wall, and more importantly it is inconspicuous, so suits all types of property. Always buy long, screw-threaded vine-eyes to take the wires further away from the wall, allowing plenty of air to circulate.

THINKING ABOUT FENCES Choosing fencing is often dictated by the budget available, but it is important to think in the long term. Putting fencing up takes the same amount of effort regardless of how much the materials cost. Most people plump for lap fencing because it is the cheapest, but the more expensive close-board panels last

Decorative, shaped trellis adds to the overall picture in the garden and can be used to emphasize a theme or create atmosphere.

longer, look better and are much stronger. With both these types of fence you will also need to put up wires stretched between vine-eyes to give your climbers something to cling on to or twine their tendrils around.

A more relaxed approach that can be very successful is to use shorter fencing panels and top them with trellis. This gives a much lighter, open feel to the garden and provides plenty of space for climbers. Alternatively, try full-height trellis, fixed between supporting posts: climbers quickly cover it and need no extra support, making it a very cost-effective solution. This works particularly well where evergreens such as ivy (*Hedera*) are used to create a slimline boundary screen.

For shorter fences try traditional picket fence, either in natural wood or perhaps painted white (a plastic version never looks right). It creates a country atmosphere. In rural areas, a random split wood fence is very effective.

(continued on page 27)

TYPES OF TRELLIS

Trellis comes in many different types. Folding trellis is suitable only for very light plants such as annual climbers. It will not be strong enough to support permanent planting. Rigid trellis is sold in different weights; generally, choose the heavier weight for free-standing trellis and the lighter version for walls. In the heavier weight there are two finishes: rough sawn and planed. Planed trellis looks much smarter but the price tag reflects this. It is, however, easier to paint and will save some money on wood treatments since it absorbs a lot less than rough-sawn timber. Rough sawn, however, is just as strong and is fine for all uses.

Recycled plastic trellises are also available. These need no preservative treatment, but they have none of the charm of the wooden version; they are also brittle, easily breaking when you try to drill them.

Choosing the right support is just as important as choosing the right climber or wall shrub. This metal pergola (above), supporting *Clematis* 'Purpurea Plena Elegans', has simple, unfussy lines and suits a modern setting, while this wooden handwoven arbour (left) is perfect for a more rustic garden.

BUYING ARCHES AND PERGOLAS

Take your time when buying a structure such as an arch or pergola for your garden, as there are a number of factors that need to be considered. If it is in kit form, is it easy to assemble or will you need professional help? How much of the structure needs to be below ground to keep it steady? Will it need concrete foundations? Is the timber treated or the metal rustproof? What annual maintenance will it need? What is its expected life span? How long is it guaranteed for?

The size and scale of the structure are especially important. Check that it is tall enough for the climbers you plan to use and that you will be able to stand or walk easily beneath it when the plants are in full growth and flower. Make sure, too, that it will be strong enough to cope with the full weight of the plants when they mature.

GARDEN FEATURES Structures like arbours, obelisks, pergolas and arches come in myriad different forms today. So how do you choose? The first rule, again, is appropriateness to the setting. For modern styles, look for a feature with simple, clean lines in materials to match those already in your garden. If you have a decking area, then use wooden features to echo the warmth and take it right into the planting. If your garden is rustic, choose features with a strong natural feel. Willow and unpeeled wood are perfect. For a more sophisticated country house look, metal finishes such as wrought iron and plastic-coated metal are very effective. For a period house, try to stick to the styles of the time.

PLANTING STEP BY STEP

Before planting, fill a bucket with water. It must be deep enough so that the pot can be fully submerged. Put your plant, still in its container, in the water and push it under the surface, holding it there until all the air bubbles have come to the top. Leave the plant to take this water into its system for a further 15 minutes. Then lift it out and allow it to drain.

PREPARING THE SITE Meanwhile, start to prepare the site for your plant. If starting a new garden it is advisable to have pre-dug the ground to remove any rubbish and to break up the soil. In established gardens you will have to make do with digging the largest hole you can fit in between the existing planting. Ideally, you need to dig a hole 20cm (8in) larger overall than the plant's rootball. Once all the soil is removed, break up the bottom of the hole with a fork to ensure water is able to drain freely.

USING PLANTING COMPOST Next mix the soil from the hole with a planting compost. This is specially

---

CHOOSING A FERTILIZER

Most plants require additional nutrients in the form of fertilizers to produce healthy leaves and shoots, roots, and flowers or fruit. Fertilizers are made up of varying proportions of three main nutrients, each serving a particular purpose: nitrogen (N) aids healthy growth of leaves and shoots; phosphates (P) encourage strong roots; and potassium or potash (K) boosts flowering and fruiting. Better-quality products also include minerals and trace elements. There are three systems for delivering this feed.

Quick-release This kind of fertilizer is bought as a powder and mixed up to a liquid form, which is very quickly available to plants. It can even be applied as a foliar feed, to be taken in through the leaves. It does not last for more than a few days in the soil and so needs constant reapplication. It may appear to be the cheapest option but rarely is, because of the large amount needed. It is useful for giving flagging plants a quick boost and works well with annual climbers.

Slow-release The commonest form of fertilizer, it can be in a powder or pelleted form and slowly breaks down in the soil, releasing food as it does so. At its worst this is a cheap and sometimes badly balanced form of food; at its best it can be a very effective way of supplying all the nutrients a plant needs. The main disadvantage of slow-release fertilizer is that it can be wasteful, since it releases food regardless of the conditions, even when there is insufficient warmth for plant growth.

Controlled-release A technologically advanced fertilizer, sold in the form of pellet-like 'prills', this consists of a liquid within a permeable polymer membrane. The membrane releases food only when there is enough moisture in the soil and enough warmth for plant growth. This stops roots getting burned by the fertilizer when the soil is dry. It also means that the fertilizer is very economical to use. It is available in different formulations, feeding for anything from one month to a year. For permanent planting, a six-month to one-year formulation is the best choice.

designed to have the correct texture to encourage strong root growth and also contains a slow-release fertilizer to feed the plant for its first six months. You can mix up your own planting mixture using peat alternative or well-composted garden material, and add a good slow- or controlled-release fertilizer. Don't plant with bonemeal: it will not harm your plant but its only purpose is to encourage initial root growth; after that it has no real benefit for your plant, providing no other nutrients. A balanced fertilizer will encourage root growth equally well, while also triggering foliage and flower production and boosting plant health and hardiness. Many gardeners only ever fertilize a plant once, so this quality all-round feed is vital for a really good start.

Backfill the hole with the planting mixture then remove a section just large enough for the pot to fit in. If adding canes for support, then do this before putting the plant in, to avoid damage to the delicate root system. Remove the climber carefully from its pot. Large specimens are often better cut from their pots to avoid root damage.

PLACING THE PLANT   Plants should never have their roots teased out: far from helping the climber get underway, it will actually harm the plant, hindering its establishment and damaging the fine root ends that take up water and feed. Place the plant carefully in the hole, making sure that the compost surface is at the same height as the natural soil level. Backfill the hole, then firm the soil around the plant with the heel of your hand. Resist the temptation to use your foot to do this. It will only compact the ground, stopping air and moisture from reaching the plant.

Leave any canes in the rootball in place: they will help mark the position of the plant and protect it from accidental damage. Remove any ties holding the plant onto the canes. You will need to do some initial training to help the climber grow in the right direction and cover its support well. For guidance see box 'Tying in new stems', below, and page 35.

WATERING   Now water the plant well, to help settle the compost around the plant. Add a thick layer of garden compost or a proprietary mulch to within 8cm (3in) of the stem to help keep the roots cool and moist.

Watering is vital during the first season. Make sure that you water close to the stem, remembering that all the plant's feeding roots are still in the ball of compost. A flush of new growth indicates that the roots are beginning to become established. Water throughout the first year.

LONG-TERM CARE   Don't forget your climber once it has settled in: feed it every spring, and again in late summer if it is greedy. Add an annual mulch every spring, and water in dry weather. Check the ties annually to make sure that they are not cutting into the plant; always loosen them before they do so. A wire tie left on a plant can be the cause of death many years later by creating a weakness low in the stem.

TYING IN NEW STEMS

When a climber is newly planted you will need to detach it from its canes and untangle the stems, training them out to cover as wide an area as possible. Wisteria is an exception to this rule. If you want it to form a sculptural, twisted, gnarled trunk, bend and curl the stems around one another and tie them in place for a season to allow them to set into this new shape.

However you train your climbers, they will need to be tied securely to their supports, at least initially. To avoid damaging the stems, all tying materials need either to expand, like stretchy plastic ones, or to degrade over a period of time, like raffia.

PLANTING CLEMATIS

Dig a hole that is large enough to accommodate the whole rootball of the clematis.

Put some planting compost or organic matter in the bottom of the hole.

Remove the pot carefully without disturbing the roots as this hinders new root growth.

Plant the clematis, checking that the compost level is no more than 8cm (3in) below soil level.

Leave the canes in and angle them towards the wall to help protect the fragile stems.

If you have not used planting compost then add some controlled-release fertilizer.

Backfill the hole with soil mixed with more planting compost or organic matter.

Water thoroughly in order to help the soil settle around the delicate root hairs.

Most gardeners would advise you to plant clematis deeply, since this gives the best chance of surviving the dreaded clematis wilt (see page 63). The truth is that while deep planting can be a great help for some clematis, it can spell death to others.

Clematis with thick, bootlace-type roots, such as the large-flowered hybrids, will benefit from deep planting. Remove all leaves up to 10cm (4in) up the stem with a sharp pair of secateurs and plant with up to 8cm (3in) of the stem below ground level. Never plant any deeper than this otherwise you may actually increase the chances of infection by placing vulnerable, less hardened stems under the soil where the fungus that causes clematis wilt lives.

Clematis with fine fibrous roots, such as *Clematis cirrhosa*, need planting with the compost level in line with the ground level. If you plant them any deeper, disease will enter through the buds below ground.

It is a common belief that clematis need their roots shaded, and gardeners are often advised to pile stones around the base of the plant in order to achieve this. In fact this actually encourages wilt, as it buries more of the plant underground, making it more vulnerable to infection. Planting a small shrub at the base of the clematis, echoing the way it grows in the wild, will both keep the roots cool and help retain moisture in the soil, something clematis love.

PLANTING CLIMBERS AGAINST A HOUSE WALL

Planting any climber or wall shrub against a house wall does have its drawbacks. Not only do the eaves stop water reaching the soil at the base of the wall, but the brickwork also absorbs any moisture that does make it into the ground. Plant the rootball at least 30cm (12in) away from the base of the wall.

Having planted away from the wall, it is then important to get the climber safely to its chosen support. Clematis and softer-stemmed plants are vulnerable: a cane or two to marking the base of the plant and angled towards the support should prevent any accidental damage. A woody-stemmed climber can just be tilted towards the wall.

A damp course stops moisture travelling up the walls and into the house. Identify it before planting and make sure that the soil does not extend above it. If the soil is already higher than the damp course, digging a narrow trench next to the wall and replacing the soil with gravel may help minimize any problems.

Pruning and training

Correct pruning can tame even the most unmanageable wisteria, bring clematis blooms back down to eye level and coax the shyest rose into flower. Understanding the reasoning behind pruning will mean that you will have no need to reach for a pruning book in future: the action required will be immediately obvious. Add to this store of knowledge the training methods that encourage the fullest flower production and your garden will be filled with colour and perhaps even fruit.

Correct pruning will give you more flowers, control over-exuberant growth and keep plants healthy and vigorous. It can even be used to alter the flowering time of climbers.

WHY PRUNING WORKS

Plants are programmed to grow, flower and set seed. They have emergency mechanisms in case something happens to disrupt this process. Pruning takes advantage of this. When the main growing shoot (or leader) is damaged (or removed by pruning) dormant buds lower down are triggered into action, replacing the one shoot with several new ones. The most vigorous will eventually become the new main shoot. The worse the damage (or harder the pruning), the stronger the new growth will be, because the root system is used to supporting a much larger plant and can regenerate very effectively. This is the key to getting the response you want when pruning. Hard pruning will produce very strong regrowth, while lighter pruning will have less dramatic results.

Pruning is a man-made art; in nature plants survive perfectly well without the constant attention of secateurs and loppers. So why do we do it?

Pruning is intended to make plants perform better. It can give us more flowers, larger blooms, a more compact habit or a reduced risk of disease, depending on how and when it is done. If this seems rather complex, then follow one simple rule: always prune immediately after flowering. For 'immediately' read 'as the majority of flowers are fading', not two months later. If you stick to this rule, you will not go far wrong.

PRUNING FOR FLOWERS The technique known as spur pruning is used to encourage flowering and fruiting. In summer, new shoots are lightly pruned to remove unnecessary leafy growth, allowing light and air to reach the potential flower buds. It also redirects the plant's food stores from growth to bud production. It is followed in winter by another light prune when the dormant flowering buds are seen.

PRUNING TO CONTROL GROWTH If a climber or wall shrub has outgrown its space by a small amount, light pruning (cutting back the new growth) can be used to bring it back under control. If it has outgrown it more dramatically, consider replacing it with a plant more suitable for the space. Hard pruning (see below) will not solve this problem; it will either encourage even stronger growth or kill the plant altogether.

Climbers trained into formal shapes also need pruning to keep them within their allocated space and shape.

PRUNING TO REJUVENATE Hard pruning, cutting back into the old, woody branches, encourages the production of growth hormones that trigger strong, leafy shoots. While some climbers can successfully be cut hard back, some will resent it and die. Try cutting back one shoot severely and see how the plant reacts before pruning the rest. Often climbers that will respond well have green buds showing at the base of the stems.

Training rose stems as near to horizontal as possible encourages a well-shaped plant, such as this *Rosa* 'Zéphirine Drouhin', with plenty of flowering shoots.

PRUNING TO ALTER THE TIME OF FLOWERING There may be occasions when you want to alter the time that a climber flowers: you may always be away on holiday when it blooms or you may have a special event for which you want it to be in flower. This involves pruning harder or later than usual, causing the plant to take longer to grow back and reach flowering point, or pruning more lightly to give earlier flowers. It works best with plants that normally flower repeatedly through the season.

REMOVING DEAD, DYING AND DISEASED WOOD When pruning you should always remove completely any growth that is dead or showing signs of dying or disease. Removing this wood first gives you a clearer view of the plant. Dead and dying growth is relatively simple to identify. 'Diseased' refers to the wood itself, not the foliage. Diseased wood cannot be cured, while disease on foliage is usually transitory. Removing the diseased wood controls problems like canker and coral spot.

BUYING SECATEURS

When buying secateurs only ever invest in the best you can afford. Cheap secateurs will be made of inferior metal and will not hold their cutting edge; they are also often badly designed and may lead to muscular strain if used regularly or for long periods. If you are using secateurs for extended periods choose a pair with rolling handles; they may feel awkward initially but you will soon get used to them.

If money is short then it is better to buy the least expensive pair of a quality brand rather than an expensive pair of a cheaper, top-selling brand. Choose the kind that can be dismantled, enabling them to be serviced easily. Never buy secateurs with stainless steel blades. These do not hold an edge at all and are a complete waste of money.

THE PRUNING CUT

Always make a pruning cut just above a bud, taking care that you are neither too close, when the bud will die, nor too far away, when the wood above the bud will die back, allowing disease into the plant.

On stems where the buds are arranged alternately, such as with roses, make the cut at 45° to the stem and sloping away from the bud. Where buds are in opposite pairs, such as with clematis, make the cut at 90° to the stem.

A SIMPLE GUIDE TO PRUNING CLIMBERS AND WALL SHRUBS

The following is a simple rule-of-thumb guide to pruning climbers and wall shrubs; there will always be exceptions, but it gives a good starting point. Clematis, roses and wisteria are dealt with separately, on the following pages. Where appropriate, extra guidance on specific pruning needs is given under the plant's main entry in the book.

SPRING FLOWERING

e.g. *Camellia × williamsii*, *Forsythia suspensa* (1)
Spring-flowering climbers and wall shrubs seldom need pruning, unless they have outgrown their allotted space. The flowers appear very early, and the plant then produces new growth that will carry flowers the following year. It is important to cut the plant back before the new growth begins. If you leave it too late you will remove the next year's flower buds. Cut back as far as is needed to keep the plant in check, and if possible cut back to plump buds or vigorous new shoots.

EARLY SUMMER FLOWERING

e.g. *Jasminum officinale*, *Lonicera periclymenum*
As with spring-flowering climbers, the growth produced after flowering carries the next year's flower buds. Pruning is usually needed only to control growth. Cut back the flowered shoots as necessary immediately after flowering, to where vigorous new shoots are emerging or buds are breaking, and occasionally remove an old shoot completely to rejuvenate the plant.

LATE SUMMER FLOWERING

e.g. *Campsis radicans*, *Passiflora caerulea*
Late-flowering climbers need the spring and summer to produce the new growth that will carry the flower buds. Plants may be cut back every year to a small main framework to stop them getting too large. This can be done at any stage between early winter, after they have finished flowering, and the start of growth in early spring. Because they may need annual pruning, some of these climbers may not be good for covering eyesores.

WINTER FLOWERING AND EVERGREEN

e.g. *Jasminum nudiflorum*, *Camellia sasanqua*
These very rarely need pruning. If you need to control growth then it is best to cut plants back as necessary in very early spring.

GRAPE VINES (*VITIS*)

Grape vines (2) are pruned with the spur system used for wisteria (see page 34). In summer, cut back shoots to five leaves. In winter, shorten these back to two buds; this has to be done in early winter, when the plants are fully dormant; if you leave it until midwinter, when the buds are swelling, the wounds will weep, weakening the plant and exposing it to disease.

ANNUAL CLIMBERS

e.g. *Lathyrus odoratus*, *Cobaea scandens*
Annual climbers simply need some attention in the very early stages of life. As the seedlings become established, regular pinching out of the tips will encourage bushy growth and more stems to carry more flowers. Later in the season, removing faded blooms (deadheading) will help divert the plant's energy into producing more flowers.

PRUNING CLEMATIS

Pruning of clematis probably causes the most confusion. In fact it is very simple. Clematis fit into three main groups. Group 1 flower early, in winter, spring and early summer, on shoots produced in the previous year; they need little pruning other than to restrict growth. Group 3 flower late, from midsummer to autumn, on the new shoots, and need hard pruning. Those that are left fall into Group 2, flowering first in spring and early summer on shoots produced in the previous year then, in mid- and late summer, on new growth; they need only a light tidy-up after the first couple of years.

GROUP 1

Year 1 – Cut back all stems to 30cm (12in) in late winter to encourage branching.

Year 2 – Cut back all stems after flowering to 1m (40in) to encourage branching higher up the plant.

Year 3 (and in subsequent years) – Cut out only dead or damaged wood and shorten stems to restrict size of plant.

GROUP 2

Year 1 – Cut back all stems to 30cm (12in) in late winter to encourage branching.

Year 2 – Cut back all stems in late winter to 1m (40in) to encourage branching higher up the plant.

Year 3 (and in subsequent years) – Cut back all stems to a strong, plump pair of buds; remove any dead and weak stems.

GROUP 3

Year 1 – Cut back all stems to 30cm (12in) in late winter to encourage branching.

Year 2 – Cut back all stems in late winter to 45cm (18in) to encourage branching higher up the plant.

Year 3 (and in subsequent years) – Cut back all stems in late winter to 45–75cm (18–30in).

PRUNING ROSES

There are two main types of roses used as climbers and they need quite different pruning treatment. When planting either, always train the shoots out horizontally to help cover the support and encourage the production of flower buds (see page 35).

RAMBLING ROSES

Ramblers (left) produce lots of new shoots from ground level. To stop the plant becoming overcrowded, simply cut back one third of the old flowering shoots to ground level after flowering. Be careful when removing the stems as they can become tangled in the new growth and damage it. Generally, rambling roses are the largest-growing and most vigorous roses.

CLIMBING, SHRUB AND MINIATURE CLIMBING ROSES

Climbing, shrub and miniature climbing roses need to build up a framework of flowering wood (see page 35). Once the framework fills the allotted space, annually cutting back shoots that have flowered to three or four buds will stimulate the growth of new flowering shoots. Occasionally cutting out an entire stem keeps the rose young and vigorous. The only other pruning necessary is a light trim to tidy up spindly or damaged growth. Pruning in midwinter, when the plant is fully dormant, is the preferred time. If the name of your climber is prefixed with the word 'climbing', as in *Rosa* 'Climbing Ena Harkness', it is a climbing sport of a bush rose. It is very important not to cut such roses hard back when they are young since they will revert to a bush form. Of all roses used as climbers, these tend to be the most appropriate size for gardens today.

PRUNING WISTERIA

Wisterias flower on short shoots (spurs) coming from the main stems. These build up to large clusters in time but need some help to encourage flower buds to form. An initial prune in midsummer removes any excess growth, allowing the plant to concentrate on producing flower buds; it also allows sunlight to reach the branches, helping to ripen the wood. A second prune in midwinter tidies up the spurs, allowing you to trim back to the plumper flower buds.

Year 1 – Train five or six vigorous shoots horizontally across the area to be covered. These are called laterals.

Year 2 – Continue to train laterals if more are needed. In midsummer reduce vertical growths from the laterals to 30cm (12in) (summer pruning).

Year 3 (and in subsequent years) – In midwinter prune the summer-pruned 30cm (12in) shoots to five or six buds. In midsummer reduce vertical growths from the laterals to 30cm (12in).

CREATING A STANDARD WISTERIA

Year 1 – Choose a strong vertical stem to use as the leader and tie it to a strong stake. Use three or four ties up the stem to ensure that it stays straight. Remove any other stems. Train the leader up to the height you require. Bear in mind that this needs to be to the final height of the top of the head of the standard, not just to the top of the stem. In midsummer cut all new growths, except the main stem, back by one third.

Year 2 – In midwinter, cut all side growths back to 6cm (2–3in). In midsummer, shorten all side growths to 30cm (12in). Leaving the side-shoots on the main stem at this point helps it to thicken up.

Year 3 (and in subsequent years) – In midwinter, shorten all growths to 6cm (2–3in). In midsummer, remove all the shoots up the stem and cut the shoots on the developing head back to 30cm (12in).

For a really special effect you can leave several stems on the plant and plait or twist them together around the support. The pruning is otherwise the same.

THE BENEFITS OF DEADHEADING

Because a plant's sole aim in life is to reproduce, it tends to cease flowering when it has produced a seedhead. In many plants, removing this seedhead triggers a new flush of flower. Even if new flowers are not produced, deadheading can still be an advantage as the plant's energy is channelled into producing new growth instead. There are a few climbers that produce decorative seedheads, such as *Clematis* 'Early Sensation' and *Cobaea scandens*, and these should be left to develop as normal.

TRAINING CLIMBERS AND WALL SHRUBS

When a climber is newly planted, the gardener's aim is to encourage it to cover as much space as quickly as possible. Once you have detached the climber from its cane, don't be tempted to train all the stems vertically. Growing shoots are programmed to develop against gravity: train them vertically and each stem will grow just one new shoot from the terminal bud, meaning you cover only a narrow area. Training stems horizontally will not only help the climber cover a much wider area, it also encourages the production of flower buds (see box, below).

On walls and fences, train climbers with flexible stems into a shallow fan shape, as near to horizontal as possible, and several new shoots will develop all along each stem; these should be fanned out above the old ones. For pergolas, obelisks and other garden features, tie the stems around the support in a spiral fashion, again training them as near to horizontal as you can. Doing this well initially means there is a sensible framework to cut back to in later years, should rejuvenation be required. Tie the growth in as and when you need to, and check the ties every year in the spring.

Plants that tend to have one or two main woody shoots (usually but not exclusively wall shrubs) need to have them tied in vertically, but the side-shoots should be tied in at an angle, as close to horizontal as possible.

In the early stages of training any climber or wall shrub, it may be necessary to remove stems that are growing away from the wall or across another stem to allow the plant to concentrate its effort on the branches you do want to keep. You may be able to reposition young, flexible stems; if not, cut them right back to the point where they emerge from the main stem.

TRAINING FOR FLOWERS

When plant stems are growing upwards, they concentrate all their growth hormones at the top of the shoot, in order to produce further upward growth. If the shoot tip gets damaged, dormant buds lower down develop and replace it. If for some reason the stem moves into a horizontal position, hormone production moves from the top of the shoot to the dormant buds. At this horizontal angle these do not develop into growth buds, but instead become flowering shoots.

In the wild, this horizontal growth usually occurs only as the plant matures and moves into a reproductive phase. So by training stems horizontally we are tricking the plant into believing that it is maturing and should be flowering.

Horizontal training of plants (here, *Stauntonia hexaphylla*) triggers hormone changes that result in an increased production of flowering shoots.

TWO'S COMPANY

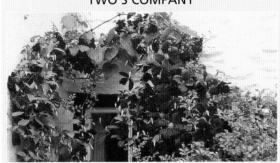

Training two climbers together is simple and effective. The woodiest climber is usually tied into position first, using the same training technique as when planted alone. It may even be a mature plant already *in situ*. The partner climber is then trained, again using the normal training technique. Often the host plant will act as a support for the partner, meaning little tying in is necessary. The climbers can share the same planting hole or, on walls for example, they can be planted at either end of the space to be filled and allowed to grow towards one another.

SITUATIONS

All gardens present various situations that offer different growing conditions. Sun-baked walls and shady corners are perfect for exotics or lush greenery. High walls provide space for more unusual climbers while low walls can be cleverly planted with combinations that will give a longer season of interest. From tender beauties for sheltered gardens and conservatories, to compact characters to grow in pots on a patio, and whether draped over garden features or used as ground cover, there is a climber for every situation.

RIGHT: *Clematis* 'Madame Julia Correvon' and *Rosa* 'Constance Spry'.

Hot, dry and sunny sites

Sun brings out the best in many climbers, some flowering most freely in a sun-baked spot, some giving their richest colour. A hot, dry, sunny site is particularly good for more tender, exotic climbers. The soil at the base of walls and structures such as pergolas is usually well drained because of foundations and rubble buried there. This is ideal for climbers and wall shrubs that dislike cold, wet soil at the roots in winter.

Hot, dry and sunny walls really lend themselves to exotic planting. Wall shrubs like the lobster claw, *Clianthus puniceus*, a native of New Zealand, thrive in the heat and look magnificent.

Abutilon × suntense 'Jermyns'

Abutilon vitifolium 'Tennant's White'

Abeliophyllum distichum, an unusual, white, forsythia-like shrub, produces fragrant, pink-flushed white flowers along the bare purplish stems in late winter (see page 149). It is very hardy but needs a warm, sunny wall to give of its best. It is an excellent plant for small gardens, slowly reaching 1.5m (5ft) in height, and with purple foliage in hot autumns.

The large, shrubby, evergreen *Abutilon × suntense* 'Jermyns'♀ thrives in hot, dry, sunny conditions. A good plant for a new garden, it grows really quickly when young, reaching a height of 4.5m (15ft). The clear mauve flowers are produced on felty silver branches over a very long period from late spring to midsummer. All this flower power takes its toll and

AVOIDING WATERLOGGING

A free-draining site is essential for many sun-loving climbers. If you suspect that water may linger in winter, perhaps because the soil is very compacted, dig out the usual planting hole then break up the bottom to allow water to drain through. Adding coarse grit to heavy soil will help to ensure that the ground drains freely.

MORE CLIMBERS WITH ATTRACTIVE FOLIAGE FOR SUNNY WALLS *Acacia baileyana* 'Purpurea' •

consequently the plant is short-lived. For a white colour scheme choose *Abutilon vitifolium* 'Tennant's White'♥. Slightly smaller, it grows to 3m (10ft), and starts flowering earlier, from mid-spring to midsummer. It makes a fabulous host for a late-flowering clematis.

Ampelopsis are not usually thought of for a sunny wall but in fact they all colour best in sun. One distinctive variety is *Ampelopsis brevipedunculata* var. *maximowiczii* 'Elegans'. It has small, vine-like leaves handsomely splashed pink and white, on rich pink stems right through the season until leaf fall. It uses tendrils to climb, so you will need to provide trellis or a wire framework for these to twine around.

Having so little green leaf, the plant is decidedly lacking in vigour. This makes it the perfect choice for small spaces, such as a tiny courtyard, or for growing in a pot. It does have small green flowers in late summer, followed occasionally by

Ampelopsis brevipedunculata var. maximowiczii 'Elegans'

blue fruit in extremely hot seasons. In a well-chosen spot it will eventually reach a height of 3m (10ft).

The trumpet vine, *Campsis radicans*, is a glamorous native of North America, with bold, pinnate, deciduous foliage and large, trumpet-shaped, rich scarlet and orange flowers at the ends of the shoots in late summer and early autumn.

started. Lead-headed nails are ideal on brick walls; for wooden structures, use plain nails each with a tie attached and slipped round the stem. Once established, campsis supports itself and makes wonderful camouflage for ugly buildings. It is also a perfect companion for climbing roses. *Campsis radicans* f. *flava* is rich yellow (see Good Companions, page 41); *Campsis radicans* 'Atrosanguinea' has large, deep reddish-scarlet flowers; 'Flamenco' is red with an orange-shaded throat; and 'Indian Summer' is rich apricot with a deeper centre.

Campsis radicans

Campsis × tagliabuana 'Madame Galen'

MANAGING SHORT-LIVED CLIMBERS

Climbers that like a hot, dry, sunny situation are very often short-lived. They grow quickly, flower profusely over a long period, then die. Have a strategy at the time of planting to ensure that your climber performs for as long as possible.

Make sure the ground is well drained; cold, wet soil in winter is almost guaranteed to force the plant to make an early exit.

Prune immediately after flowering; this encourages the plant to put its energy into growth rather than into seed production.

Take cuttings when you feel the plant is looking at its peak; following seasons will see a decline in vigour. Cuttings are easy (see page 19) and the young plants establish quickly.

In the wild it scrambles up trees and reaches up to 14m (46ft); in gardens it is smaller, growing to 10m (33ft). The name *campsis*, from *kampe* meaning 'bending', refers to its habit of turning its growth towards potential supports. For such an exotic-looking flower it is surprisingly hardy, and will survive a few degrees of frost as long as it has the benefit of a sunny, sheltered site.

Although self-clinging with the aid of aerial roots, it needs some help getting

Campsis grandiflora has even more spectacular flowers, but sadly it is rather more tender. *Campsis* × *tagliabuana* 'Madame Galen'♥ is a hardier hybrid of the two species. It has looser trusses of salmon-red flowers from late summer to early autumn, when the leaves fall. It is vigorous and reaches 10m (33ft), but is not as good at clinging to its support, so careful tying in is needed.

Usually wall shrubs need to be tied in to a support framework, but *Carpenteria*

Carpenteria californica

Magnolia grandiflora 'Goliath'

californica♚ is one that positively dislikes this treatment. Grow it next to a wall rather than against it. Sometimes called the tree anemone, it is better described as an evergreen philadelphus, to which genus it is allied. The scented, white flowers, produced in early to midsummer, are 8cm (3in) across, with golden anthers. Reaching 3m (10ft) in all directions, this shrub is most suitable for larger gardens because the evergreen foliage can look a little shabby after the flowers have finished. The species itself tends to be very variable so always buy a named variety. 'Elizabeth' has dense clusters of flowers, but 'Bodnant', with larger blooms, is probably better known.

Several **clematis** prefer a position in sun. *Clematis* 'Ruby', an alpina-type hybrid (see Good Companions, right, and see page 120), positively loves it, giving a much richer colour there. In mid- to late

spring it has nodding, deep purple-pink flowers with creamy-primrose centres flushed pink on the outside; it reliably flowers again in late summer. It is a neat plant, growing to 3m (10ft).

Clianthus puniceus♚, or lobster claw, sometimes listed as *Clianthus puniceus* 'Red Cardinal', is very exotic (see page 38). This semi-evergreen shrub, 3.5m (12ft) tall, comes from North Island, New Zealand, where it is now very rare in the wild. The curiously claw-shaped flowers are brilliant red and produced in large clusters in spring and early summer. Although short-lived, it is a dramatic addition to any garden. The variety 'Albus'♚, with slightly muddy white flowers, is not worth hunting for, losing all its drama with the change in colour.

For a magnificent large, evergreen shrub for a dry, sunny wall, *Magnolia*

Clianthus puniceus

grandiflora (bull bay or southern magnolia) is unbeatable. It is classically beautiful, with glossy, rich green leaves, often with a rusty-coloured felt underside, and intensely fragrant, creamy-white flowers, 25cm (10in) wide, produced from midsummer to mid-autumn. This magnolia can grow to 15m (50ft) and so needs plenty of space.

Magnolia grandiflora 'Exmouth'♚ is the most freely available. It produces very large, richly fragrant, white flowers from an early age, unlike some other varieties, and is lime-tolerant if given deep loam soil. *Magnolia grandiflora* 'Edith Bogue' is very hardy and the best choice for colder areas. 'Victoria'♚ is distinctive with a bright red protective bract around each flower bud and a red stain on the stems. 'Goliath' is beautiful, with extra-large flowers, 30cm (12in) across, but is relatively scarce in cultivation.

If choosing a climber for the back of a hot, dry, sunny border then the semi-evergreen *Solanum crispum* 'Glasnevin'♚ (see Good Companions, right) must be near the top of the list. The bright purple, star-shaped flowers with tiny, bright yellow beaks are produced very freely all through summer and into autumn. For sheer flower power this plant is extremely hard to beat.

'Glasnevin' is vigorous and easy to grow; it is not fussy about soil, and even loves chalk. It is said to dislike cold, but seems to survive all but the worst of winters quite happily given good drainage at the roots. A large, shrubby grower, this scrambling climber reaches 6m (20ft) tall

Clematis 'Ruby'

Magnolia grandiflora

MORE CLIMBERS AND SHRUBS FOR SUNNY WALLS *Aristolochia macrophylla* • *Ceanothus* 'Autumnal Blue' •

Solanum crispum 'Glasnevin'

Solanum laxum 'Album'

Solanum laxum 'Album Variegatum'

and, if left to its own devices, 4m (13ft) across, and so needs plenty of space in front. If planting it against an open fence make sure that the neighbours do not mind it in their garden, too, otherwise keep it to a solid background.

With a delicate, slender habit, **Solanum laxum 'Album'**♛ is a good choice for smaller gardens. Yellow-beaked white flowers are produced in loose, elegant clusters from midsummer to the frosts. The semi-evergreen foliage is a good dark green, often flushed with a hint of purple. It grows to 3m (10ft).

There is also a variegated variety called **Solanum laxum 'Album Variegatum'**, with the same white flowers. The delicate leaves have a rich golden edge and look stunning on a trellis screen when the sun shines through, lighting up the foliage. Its only fault is a tendency to some winter damage, but affected stems are easily cut out in spring and new shoots quickly replace them.

Stauntonia hexaphylla is a strong, evergreen, twining climber closely related to *Holboellia* (see page 121). Given a hot, dry, sunny wall, it produces violet-tinged white flowers in spring, followed in a hot summer by egg-shaped, purple-tinged, pulpy fruit, which are edible. Growing to 10m (33ft), it is not a plant for small spaces; in a larger garden, it would make a superb host for a sun-loving clematis such as the rich, deep velvety-blue *Clematis* 'Lady Betty Balfour' (see page 112).

Trachelospermum asiaticum♛ is now beginning to receive the praise it deserves. In mid- and late summer, the

Stauntonia hexaphylla

elegant evergreen foliage is starred with creamy-white, richly scented flowers (see page 81). This twining climber loves a hot, sunny site and will succeed in all but the coldest localities, being hardier than its close relative *Trachelospermum jasminoides*♛ (see page 96). In many cases it also makes a more satisfactory choice than the summer jasmine, *Jasminum officinale*♛ (see page 127). Although it eventually reaches 6m (20ft) in height, it has a neat, compact shape that is much more suited to smaller gardens and it is more inclined to mix with other climbing plants than to swamp them. There is also a golden-leaved variety called **'Golden Memories'** (see page 103).

GOOD COMPANIONS

Rosa 'Madame Alfred Carrière'♛ (1) makes an excellent host for the rich yellow flowers of *Campsis radicans* f. *flava* (2). Between them they will flower all through summer and into early autumn.

Grow *Convolvulus cneorum*♛ (3) at the foot of the alpina-type hybrid *Clematis* 'Ruby' (4): both plants thoroughly enjoy hot, sunny conditions.

Euphorbia characias subsp. *wulfenii* 'John Tomlinson'♛ (5) is bold enough to contrast with the mass of flowers on *Solanum crispum* 'Glasnevin'♛ (6).

Fallopia baldschuanica • *Jasminum* × *stephanense* • *Passiflora caerulea* • *Rosa* 'Guinée' • *Wisteria floribunda* •

Shady sites

Many climbers do well in shady sites. They may simply be very tolerant plants, growing as well in extreme shade and dry soil as they do in any other situation, or they may need shade because they must have a cool, moist root run. Other climbers grow happily in any position, but their flower or foliage colour is bleached by sun and so they are best seen in shade.

Camellia × williamsii 'Donation'

Camellias (see page 117) are extremely happy in shade. The large, leathery leaves cope well with low light levels. The one thing they do need is consistent watering. If the soil dries out in late summer, the flower buds will not form properly and will later drop. Adding organic matter when planting will help the soil retain moisture. All varieties of *Camellia japonica* and *Camellia × williamsii* will do well on shady walls, reaching 9m (30ft) and 5m (16ft) respectively. Flowering time is from mid- to late spring, a little earlier if on a relatively warm wall. White flowers especially do well on shady walls.

Striped **clematis** hybrids need a shady wall to stop the flower colour becoming bleached. These varieties tend to be sniffed at for being vulgar. Look more

Camellia flowers develop brown patches if exposed to early morning sun after a frosty night, white flowers suffering especially badly. The shelter of a shady wall allows *Camellia japonica* 'Alba Simplex' (left) and *Camellia × williamsii* 'Donation' (above) to open their gorgeous blooms without harm.

CAMELLIAS FOR SHADY WALLS

Camellia japonica **cultivars**
'Guilio Nuccio'♥ (1) Very large, salmon-red blooms; long-flowering, from late winter to early summer.

'Margaret Davis Picotee'♥ Formal double flowers, white with a pink edge.
'Tricolor'♥ (2) White flowers with pink stripes.

Camellia × williamsii **cultivars**
'Anticipation'♥ (3) Very large, dark pinkish-red, peony-form flowers.

'Donation'♥ Pale pink blooms; the best camellia (see above).
'Jury's Yellow'♥ (4) Anemone-form, creamy-yellow flowers.

LEVELS OF SHADE

As with all garden conditions, there are degrees of shade. It can be anything from lightly dappled to a deep, chilling lack of light.

Dappled shade occurs in the shade of trees with a light canopy. Plants find it relatively easy to grow here as the light levels are fairly good. Camellias especially enjoy growing on a wall in dappled shade.

Semi- or partial shade means that the site is shaded for part of the day. The amount of shade will also vary according to the angle of the sun at different times of the year. A good many plants will grow happily here, but not those that prefer full sun.

Deep shade means an area shaded all through the day, often by a large building or tree. Generally plants with dark green, leathery leaves grow well in deep shade.

Shade is further divided into moist shade and dry shade. Moist shade is easy: most climbers that like deep shade will thrive here and have plenty of lush foliage. Dry shade is the most difficult. Adding organic matter to the soil will improve its water-holding ability. Tough climbers like ivy will grow in even the driest shade.

Clematis 'Corona'

Clematis 'John Warren'

Clematis 'Mrs N. Thompson'

Clematis 'Nelly Moser'

closely at them and you will see they consist of fabulous pearlescent jewel colours, unmatched in any other climber.

This is a surprisingly consistent group of hybrids. They have a compact, free-flowering habit, making them well suited to containers and small gardens, and they have large flowers in late spring and early summer, with another flush in late summer. Those described below grow to 2.5m (8ft) unless stated otherwise.

Clematis 'Carnaby' is exceptionally free-flowering, continuing to bloom until early autumn. The deep raspberry-pink

flowers with a deeper bar are 12cm (5in) across. It is excellent for containers. A more compact plant, reaching just 2m (6ft), *Clematis* 'Corona' has purple flowers suffused pink with orange highlights and dark red anthers. The flowers, 18cm (7in) across, are very profusely borne, making this a good plant for a small garden, really earning its space.

Clematis 'John Warren' is very different: the huge, pointed flowers, 23cm (9in) across, are greyish pink with a deeper bar and, unusually, deeper

margins and red anthers. As with all the really large-flowered hybrids, it needs a sheltered spot to avoid wind damage.

For a striped hybrid with personality *Clematis* 'Mrs N. Thompson' is an excellent choice. The scarlet-striped, deep violet flowers are smaller than most, at 12cm (5in), and can be of variable shape, but this simply adds to their charm.

Clematis 'Nelly Moser'♛, introduced in 1897 at the height of clematis breeding, is probably the most famous of all the striped hybrids, with large, cartwheel-

PETALS, SEPALS OR TEPALS?

Clematis flowers – here, *Clematis* 'Fairy Blue' (CRYSTAL FOUNTAIN) – and those of many other plants, don't strictly have petals at all. Instead, the sepals, the usually green outer covering protecting the flower bud, have adapted to look like petals, becoming petaloid sepals (also known as tepals). To make life more complicated, the stamens sometimes mutate into narrow, petal-like forms, known as petaloid stamens.

Clematis montana is unusual in that its colour fades in shade. Choose a deep pink form such as 'Freda', here planted with var. *rubens* 'Odorata', to avoid ending up with plain white flowers.

OTHER GOOD STRIPED CLEMATIS

'Barbara Dibley'	'Fair Rosamond'	'Ruby Glow' (see Good
'Barbara Jackman' (1)	'Lincoln Star'	Companions, below right)
'Bees' Jubilee' (2)	'Pink Fantasy'	'Scartho Gem' (3)
'Duchess of Sutherland'	ROYAL VELVET ('Evifour')	'Sealand Gem'

Hydrangea anomala subsp. petiolaris

Pleostegia viburnoides

shaped flowers, 20cm (8in) across, of pale pink with a carmine central bar and dark red anthers.

Clematis 'Star of India', an old hybrid introduced in 1867, is indeed a star. The flowers, 8–10cm (3–4in) across, have wide, blunt-tipped sepals in rich red-purple with a red stripe and greenish anthers. They are produced from mid- to late summer and look sensational against a light background.

Clematis montana and many of its hybrids are happy against a shady wall.

Ficus pumila

They flower from late spring to early summer and have white or pink, usually single but sometimes double flowers. They are vigorous and easy-going about soil type. (See page 123.)

The climbing fig, *Ficus pumila*♀, is an unusual choice for shade. This is a self-clinging evergreen with small, ovate, green leaves; if it is particularly happy it will produce tiny green figs, maturing to a warm plum colour, at intervals throughout the year. Despite its small leaves it will reach up to 5m (16ft) in height. It needs protection from frost.

Ivies (*Hedera*) are the perfect climbers for shade: this is their natural habitat. The evergreen, leathery leaves tolerate low light well, and the huge range of varieties growing to anything from a matter of centimetres up to 10m (33ft) means that there is one for any possible use. The variegated cultivars hold their colour in

shade and so are extremely valuable for brightening up even the darkest corner. (See pages 152–53.)

The climbing hydrangea, *Hydrangea anomala* subsp. *petiolaris*♀, is not greatly fussy; it will grow in all types of soil and on any aspect, but it does perform very well on shady walls. It is slow to become established and lead-headed nails are essential to get the stems in place. In summer, the glossy green foliage makes a superb foil for the greenish-white lacecap flowers. Even after leaf drop this climber is attractive as the sturdy, self-clinging stems are an appealing shade of russet-brown. It will reach up to 15m (50ft) on a wall and even larger grown through a tree. It is especially good in industrial or polluted areas. (See Good Companions, right.)

There is also a form called *Hydrangea anomala* subsp. *petiolaris* var. *tiliifolia*,

MORE GOOD CLIMBERS AND WALL SHRUBS FOR SHADE *Akebia quinata • Berberidopsis corallina •*

ROSES THAT WILL SURVIVE ON SHADY WALLS

'Albéric Barbier'♚	'Félicité Perpétué'♚	'Kathleen Harrop'	'Maigold'♚
'Bantry Bay'	'Gloire de Dijon' (1)	'Madame Alfred Carrière'♚	'New Dawn'♚
'Danse du Feu'	'Golden Showers'♚ (2)	'Madame Grégoire	'Veilchenblau'♚
'Ena Harkness'	'Guinée'	Staechelin'♚ (3)	'Zéphirine Drouhin' (4)

which has smaller, more refined leaves and flowers and is a little more compact, growing to 10m (33ft).

Pileostegia viburnoides♚ is an evergreen, self-clinging climber with leathery, green, strongly veined leaves. The fluffy, creamy-white flowers are produced in panicles 15cm (6in) across in late summer. It is rather slow-growing but eventually will reach 6m (20ft). It is very good on shady walls but thrives on sunny walls, too.

Roses (see pages 130–32) are renowned for liking a sunny spot. Varieties that are suggested for a shady wall do not particularly relish it, but they will survive there, although their flowering will be much weaker than in sun. If at all possible save roses for sunny walls and choose a different climber that will positively thrive in shade.

Schizophragma hydrangeoides is a Japanese native found in mountain forests, often with *Hydrangea anomala* subsp. *petiolaris*. (see above). This self-clinging, deciduous climber has large, coarsely toothed leaves, contrasting well

GOOD COMPANIONS

The rich gold in the centre of the leaves of *Hedera helix* 'Oro di Bogliasco', better known as 'Goldheart' (1), is echoed in the bright colours of pansies (2), which can be planted at the base.

For a cool planting scheme, grow *Polystichum setiferum* Divisilobum Group 'Herrenhausen' (3) with *Hydrangea anomala* subsp. *petiolaris*♚ (4). The two create a leafy green oasis.

Choisya ternata SUNDANCE ('Lich')♚ (5) is at its best in dappled shade and makes a lovely foil for the flowers of *Clematis* 'Ruby Glow' (6).

Schizophragma hydrangeoides

with the large heads of creamy-white flowers and lance-shaped, petal-like bracts borne in midsummer. It is a slow starter and will need careful attention while the aerial roots get going, but will eventually reach 12m (40ft). The leaves of *Schizophragma hydrangeoides* 'Moonlight' (see page 83) are ghostly silver with green veins and turn yellow in autumn. *Schizophragma hydrangeoides* 'Roseum'♚ is a pink-flowered form.

45

Celastrus orbiculatus · × *Fatshedera lizei* · *Muehlenbeckia complexa* · *Schisandra rubriflora* ·

Low walls

Small gardens and low walls often go together. When space is limited remember that texture and scent both come to the fore. There is no need to restrict your choice of plants to short climbers: think laterally as well – in a sense, short walls are only tall walls laid horizontally. They look fantastic with vigorous, bold climbers draped informally in swags along their length. Using two climbers together is particularly successful, the one intensifying the effect of the other. Together they may provide a colour harmony, a contrast in texture or an extended season of flower.

The dusky flowers of *Clematis* 'Hagley Hybrid' scramble informally over a charming old wall, creating a romantic atmosphere.

Clematis chrysocoma

Clematis chrysocoma is a small-flowered species clematis, perfect on a low wall, for gardeners who want something special. It is similar in flower to *Clematis montana* (see page 48), with soft pink, four-sepalled flowers, and the new growths are covered with soft golden down. It is fairly small, reaching only 2m (6ft), and flowers later than *Clematis montana*, in early to late summer. It is a little tender and needs very free-draining soil; if it were hardier, it would undoubtedly be much more widely grown.

Clematis CLAIR DE LUNE

Clematis 'Etoile de Paris'

Clematis 'Ramona'

Clematis 'Beauty of Worcester'

Large-flowered **clematis** hybrids that start flowering in spring build up a framework of stems that reach a height, or in this case spread, of 2.5m–3m (8–10ft). *Clematis* CLAIR DE LUNE ('Evirin'), sometimes known as BLUE MOON, is fantastic on a low wall. One of the best of its type, it is compact and free-flowering, producing white flowers with ruffled lilac edges almost non-stop from late spring to early autumn. In strong sun, the colour fades, but the flowers are still really attractive. (See Good Companions, page 49.)

Clematis 'Etoile de Paris' grows to just 2m (6ft) and is in bloom from late spring to early summer. The large flowers are blue-mauve, with pointed tips and red anthers. Unlike most large-flowered hybrids, it has good autumn seedheads.

For sheer reliability try *Clematis* 'Hagley Hybrid'. The flowers are of only average size, but have a very distinctive appearance, with pointed, richly textured sepals in a slightly dusky mauve-pink and dull burgundy anthers. The growth is compact, and flowers are produced in great profusion from early summer to early autumn.

This clematis makes a fine companion for roses, especially those of a rich deep colour, but if planted with pink roses their clear tone will make the clematis look muddy in comparison. 'Hagley Hybrid' will fade in strong light so is best planted out of the hot midday sun.

A clematis hybrid that will take the sun and loves the company of pale pink roses is *Clematis* 'Ramona'. The beautiful, pale blue flowers are large, up to 18cm (7in) wide, with red anthers, and are produced from early summer to early autumn. It is strong-growing, reaching 3m (10ft), and needs a sunny site for the growth from the previous year to ripen fully.

Double-flowered clematis (see pages 126 and 133) are very effective on low walls, their compact habit of 2.5m (8ft) and, often, variable flowers suiting a small space. The flowers of *Clematis* 'Belle of Woking', produced in late spring, are always double, with masses of sepals in a delicious silvery lilac colour. Although it is one of the prettiest doubles, 'Belle of Woking' has weak stems and needs to be threaded through a host plant.

Clematis 'Beauty of Worcester' is a gorgeous old variety. The flowers are a stunning dark violet-blue with contrasting milky anthers. Those produced in early and midsummer are double but still show their anthers, while those in late summer are single. It needs a sunny wall to encourage strong growth. (See Good Companions, page 49.)

Clematis 'Mrs Spencer Castle' has really unusual colouring: rich pale pink with a stronger flush at the base. While this is not the most exciting plant in mid- to late summer, when it produces single flowers, the double flowers in

FAULTY FLOWERS?

Double varieties of clematis often follow their first crop of flowers with a later bonus of single blooms, which may be quite different in shape from the original flowers. There are also some varieties that produce double, semi-double and single flowers all at the same time.

Some varieties, particularly white ones, show green patches on the flowers, especially early in the season. This can be a surprise if the flowers were all white when the plant was purchased. *Clematis* 'Duchess of Edinburgh' (see above and page 133) is one of the worst culprits in spring, while *Clematis* 'Alba Luxurians' ♀ (see page 139) has green tips to the flowers nearly all season.

Some colours are more prone to fading than others. Creamy yellow flowers and those with pink stripes are all liable to fade in bright sun. Other colours can vary according to the weather or growing conditions.

Clematis 'Veronica's Choice'

Clematis 'Warwickshire Rose'

Clematis 'Bill MacKenzie'

Smaller walls look bigger when planted with two climbers such as the self-clinging *Hedera colchica* 'Sulphur Heart' and *Euonymus fortunei* 'Emerald 'n' Gold'.

early summer are stunning. The raspberry flush gives each one an amazing depth, accentuated by the twisted sepals. Despite being slightly shy to flower, this is well worth growing if you are looking for something different.

The only double, large-flowered clematis hybrid that has scent is *Clematis* 'Veronica's Choice'. Its perfume is not overwhelming, just a delicate hint of primroses. The flowers are pale lavender flushed with rosy pink and gorgeously ruffled on the edges; they are double in early summer, and single from midsummer onwards. They hold their colour best in light shade.

Clematis montana (see page 123) is a large-growing, small-flowered species that makes fantastic cover for low walls. The cultivar **'Warwickshire Rose'** is especially effective here. Its delicately veined foliage is deep bronze when young and makes a superb foil for the beautiful, dark pink flowers. *Clematis montana* var. *rubens* 'Odorata' is also good, with almond-scented, pale pink flowers (see page 44). Both are in bloom from late spring to early summer and grow to 9m (30ft).

Clematis tangutica is another small-flowered species, growing to 6m (20ft). One of the few yellow clematis, it is wonderful for late-summer colour. The flowers are nodding, with four rich yellow sepals that appear thick like lemon peel. The best form is *Clematis* **'Bill MacKenzie'**, which has very large, bright yellow flowers, with purple filaments and greenish-tan anthers. It blooms over such a long period, from midsummer to late autumn, that the seedheads mingle freely with the flowers. It is happy in almost any soil and is easy to grow. This clematis seeds freely but does not come true from seed, so it is important to buy the plant from a reputable nursery or garden centre to ensure that you get the true vegetatively propagated variety.

Foliage colour is essential to soften walls, especially in winter when they can look quite harsh. *Euonymus fortunei* (see page 88) and its cultivars are self-clinging evergreens with boldly coloured foliage. **'Emerald 'n' Gold'** has rich green leaves edged with gold, sometimes taking on pinkish-red tones in cold weather. **'Silver Queen'** has grey-green leaves edged with cream. Once established they grow quickly and some can reach a height of 3m (10ft).

Garrya × *issaquahensis* 'Glasnevin Wine' is an attractive bushy shrub for small walls that also makes the perfect host for clematis. Growing up to 2m (6ft) tall, with a spread of 4m (13ft), it has evergreen, leathery leaves on reddish-purple new shoots; elegant, red-purple flushed catkins appear from midwinter through to early spring.

Fragrance adds a special element to small gardens and jasmine is one of the

OTHER CLIMBERS AND WALL SHRUBS FOR LOW WALLS *Abutilon* 'Kentish Belle' • *Chaenomeles japonica* •

Euonymus fortunei 'Silver Queen'

Garrya × issaquahensis 'Glasnevin Wine'

Jasminum officinale FIONA SUNRISE

most sweetly scented climbers. Combining scent with unusual foliage makes good use of your space and, although deciduous, *Jasminum officinale* FIONA SUNRISE ('Frojas'), 'Argenteovariegatum'♥ and 'Aureum' really earn their keep (see pages 102–103 and 127). All flower from summer to early autumn.

With their richly scented flowers, which are usually produced from early summer onwards, **honeysuckles** (*Lonicera*) are an excellent choice for low walls. Choose cultivars with good foliage to make the most of the space. *Lonicera similis* var. *delavayi*♥ (see page 129) has elegant, semi-evergreen foliage and large creamy flowers, ageing to honey yellow, with the most gorgeous scent. It grows to 5m (16ft). *Lonicera japonica* 'Aureoreticulata', growing to 6m (20ft), has evergreen, deep green foliage, intricately veined with delicate golden yellow, and laced with cream flowers that turn to parchment yellow as they age. The many forms of the deciduous common woodbine, *Lonicera periclymenum*, will also look wonderful on low walls. The large heads of richly scented, cream flowers are flushed with red and give a lovely cottage-garden feel. All grow to 5–7m (16–22ft). (See also pages 128–29.)

Some of the most pleasing climbers for small walls are **wisterias** (see pages 124–25). They grow large, reaching up to 9m (30ft), but can be pruned to fit a smaller space. Training and pruning (see page 34) is so much easier on a low wall, where all the growth is accessible. Varieties of *Wisteria sinensis* make the best choice as their racemes of flowers are not overlong. *Wisteria sinensis* 'Jako' has white flowers in late spring and early summer, sometimes with a lilac edge in strong sun. The name 'Jako' means musk, and this is the most strongly scented white sinensis. It is also one of the first to flower. (See Good Companions, left.) The lilac-tinted white 'Alba' and deep violet-blue 'Amethyst' are also good choices.

GOOD COMPANIONS

Dark violet-blue *Clematis* 'Beauty of Worcester' (1) looks fantastic growing through a deep red rose such as *Rosa* 'Guinée' (2), which will also enjoy a sunny spot.

Clematis CLAIR DE LUNE ('Evirin') (3) is simply gorgeous planted with a delicate pink English rose like *Rosa* EGLANTYNE ('Ausmak')♥ (4).

Wisteria sinensis 'Jako' (5) is a marvellous early-flowering host for *Clematis* 'Abundance'♥ (6), which produces masses of rich red flowers much later in the summer.

Clematis 'Countess of Lovelace' • *Coronilla valentina* subsp. *glauca* 'Citrina' • *Cotoneaster horizontalis* • *Hedera helix* •

High walls

High walls rarely mean beauty; more often they are ugly, concrete or painted edifices that desperately need softening. A self-clinging climber is the most sensible plant to use here. For other forms of climber, supports can be provided but they must be high quality, to last for a long time without maintenance. Vine-eyes and wires are the most adaptable and the least obvious, an important factor when the climber has not yet covered its allotted space.

Akebia quinata

Akebia quinata 'Cream'

followed by sausage-shaped fruit in hot summers. It loves a good, fertile soil, and although it revels in sun, it will also tolerate a shady spot. In the USA it can be invasive, overpowering local native plants. In Britain it is not a problem at all.

Left: *Parthenocissus henryana* looks gorgeous on a wall built of glowing golden Bath stone. It will soften even ugly modern walls equally effectively.

STONE HOUSE COTTAGE GARDEN

Climbers and ramblers galore run riot in this delightful brick-walled garden in Stone, near Kidderminster, Worcestershire. In the 1970s its owners, the Arbuthnotts, added towers, gazebos and minarets to the old kitchen-garden walls in order to display their collection of climbing plants. These follies are now draped with roses, clematis, wisterias, jasmines and honeysuckles, as well as countless more unusual climbers and wall shrubs.

Aristolochia macrophylla

Akebia quinata, commonly called the chocolate vine, has curious, five-lobed, dark purple, cocoa-scented flowers, borne in early spring. A big, boisterous, twining climber, reaching 10m (33ft), it is ideal for high walls. (See Good Companions, page 53.) There are two less well known cultivars with amethyst and soft cream flowers called **'Amethyst Glow'** and **'Cream'** respectively.

The foliage is five-lobed, and very like that of *Choisya* (Mexican orange blossom), and is evergreen in mild winters. Flowers are carried in groups, with male and female flowers together, and may be

MORE CLIMBERS AND WALL SHRUBS FOR HIGH WALLS *Ampelopsis brevipedunculata • Campsis grandiflora •*

Aristolochia macrophylla, commonly known as Dutchman's pipe, has remarkable flowers, shaped like an old-fashioned smoking pipe; each has a long, curving, yellow-green tube, opening up to a wide throat and turning back on itself, with a purple-brown tip. They are produced at the ends of the twining stems in early summer. It has large, handsome, deciduous foliage and grows to 10m (33ft). It will need to be given some form of support, but it is worth the effort this involves as the foliage has a long season of interest.

Celastrus orbiculatus (oriental bittersweet) is another climber that carries a warning for the USA. It is more vigorous than the native American bittersweet (*Celastrus scandens*) and is proving troublesome in the wild. In Britain, however, it makes a fabulous cover for large walls, reaching up to 14m (46ft) in height. Its twining stems carry handsome, deciduous leaves that turn rich yellow-orange in autumn, and the starry, greenish flowers, borne in summer, are followed by fruit in huge, hanging clusters. The pods turn from green to gold as they open, revealing shiny scarlet seeds within. The branches are laden with them and they remain on the plant well into winter, as birds find them unpalatable. Make sure you buy a hermaphrodite form to ensure seeds are produced.

This is a striking climber, excellent for a high wall, or to grow through a tall tree where the shoots laden with red seeds can hang elegantly down. It prefers semi- or full shade and is extremely hardy.

For a warm wall *Clematis flammula* is ideal. Whether in direct sunlight, or surrounded by buildings that radiate heat, this clematis will perform spectacularly. Reaching 5m (16ft), it makes a bushy tangle of bright green, deciduous foliage that from midsummer to mid-autumn is liberally covered with deliciously scented, small, white flowers. The scent is strong and like vanilla or almonds.

Clematis flammula

Clematis rehderiana

Clematis terniflora

Clematis × triternata 'Rubromarginata'

Clematis rehderiana♀ oozes class, with elegantly bell-shaped flowers of a subtle primrose-yellow with a hint of lime. They have the scent of cowslips, and are borne from midsummer to mid-autumn. This species is a strong grower, reaching 7m (22ft) before leaf fall, and it flowers later than many other summer clematis.

Another lesser-known clematis is *Clematis terniflora*. A vigorous plant, reaching 6m (20ft), it is well suited to a high wall, needing lots of sun if it is to flower freely. Given enough shelter it will remain evergreen, but in most places it loses its leaves. The masses of starry, white flowers last from late summer through to mid-autumn. It is a huge favourite in the warmer parts of North America, where long summers encourage an abundance of flowers. It is often known as *Clematis*

paniculata, but that name more properly belongs to a different species. *Clematis terniflora* var. *terniflora*, sometimes called *Clematis terniflora* var. *robusta*, is more vigorous, reaching 7m (22ft). The flowers have broader sepals, but still retain the starry appearance of the species.

For a more reliable performer in colder climates choose *Clematis × triternata* 'Rubromarginata'♀. It is a hybrid between the richly perfumed, late-flowering, white *Clematis flammula* and the tough, free-flowering, but scentless, purple *Clematis viticella*♀. The result is huge clouds of starry, white flowers, edged in rich, velvety purple, from midsummer to early autumn. This is one of the most attractive scented clematis. It is a very old hybrid, but has plenty of vigour, reaching 5m (16ft) before leaf fall.

Ceanothus arboreus 'Trewithen Blue' • *Clematis montana* var. *grandiflora* • *Clematis montana* var. *rubens* 'Tetrarose' •

Fallopia baldschuanica

Fallopia baldschuanica is a much maligned, twining climber, known as mile a minute or Russian vine; it really will grow extremely quickly, and reaches 15m (50ft) high. This plant is not one for a 2m (6ft) fence, no matter what the length; it is just too vigorous. Given a suitable situation, however, it makes a superb deciduous climber. It looks delightful tumbling elegantly across the face of a high wall or scrambling through a tall tree. The pointed, heart-shaped leaves are dark green, and the frothy panicles of tiny, pink-tinged, creamy-white flowers, produced in late summer, are stunning.

Ivy (*Hedera*) is the real workhorse for a high wall: self-supporting, evergreen and easy to grow in any soil, in sun or shade (see pages 152–53). Rather than reach

Hedera helix

immediately for variegated forms, spare some thought for the common English ivy, *Hedera helix*. It is vigorous, growing to 10m (33ft), resistant to pollution and has green flowers in autumn, followed by attractive green and black berries that flower arrangers love.

If looking for an ivy to clothe a high wall, do choose with care. Many

gardeners think that one ivy is as good as another, but many are either tender or very small-growing.

The tender forms hail from the Dutch houseplant trade. Each year millions of ivies are produced as houseplants and also for use as summer bedding. These are fine for growing under cover, but outside may suffer frost damage in winter. Some of our best-known varieties, *Hedera helix* 'Anna Marie', 'Glacier'♀, 'Eva' and 'Harald', fall into this category, as does *Hedera canariensis* (also known as *Hedera algeriensis*). *Hedera canariensis* 'Gloire de Marengo'♀ is popular but it is not suitable for cold walls. It will survive cold periods, but the foliage will be lost or damaged and the plant will look poor until new leaves appear in summer.

Small trailing ivies tend to be mixed with the climbing varieties when offered for sale and it can be hard to differentiate between them. *Hedera helix* 'Little Diamond', 'Spetchley'♀ and 'Très Coupé' are often seen like this. They do not climb properly, and are much happier making a low mound of growth, perhaps in a rock garden or at the front of a border (see page 73).

Both *Hedera helix* and the next climber, *Lonicera japonica,* should be treated with caution in the US. Both species are a little too successful there, causing problems in native woodlands. Use *Hedera colchica* (see page 153) and *Lonicera similis* var. *delavayi*♀ (see page 129) as alternatives; neither is quite as vigorous and these will not stray from cultivation.

The Japanese honeysuckle, **Lonicera japonica**, is a little like *Fallopia baldschuanica* (see above) in that it has been planted unwisely in the past. It is a vigorous grower, easily reaching 9m (30ft); it also roots wherever the leaf nodes touch the ground, creating countless new plants. For this reason in a small garden it is a high-maintenance plant, and there are better choices for this situation. It is recommended because it is

IVIES SUITABLE FOR LARGE WALLS

Hedera colchica♀	*Hedera colchica* 'Sulphur	*Hedera helix* 'Clotted
Hedera colchica	Heart'♀ (**2**)	Cream' (**3**)
'Dentata'♀	*Hedera helix*	*Hedera helix* 'Glymii'
Hedera colchica 'Dentata	'Atropurpurea'	*Hedera helix* 'Oro di
Variegata'♀ (**1**)	*Hedera helix* 'Caecilia'♀	Bogliasco' ('Goldheart')

OTHER CLIMBERS AND WALL SHRUBS FOR HIGH WALLS *Cytisus battandieri* • *Jasminum officinale* •

semi-evergreen and blooms from early summer right through to mid-autumn. The flowers, although relatively small, are very fragrant and on a warm summer evening this honeysuckle will scent an entire garden with its sweet perfume.

On a high wall it is ideal: the twining stems all have room to reach for the sky, the semi-evergreen foliage provides a fresh green cover, and the creamy-white and honey-yellow flowers look and smell delightful (see page 10). One last word of caution: in a spot where the roots get too dry, Japanese honeysuckle will be very prone to mildew in late summer; the plant may even lose its leaves. It will recover, however, and continue to flower.

Lonicera japonica 'Halliana'♔ is probably the best known variety and may well be the typical form of the

Lonicera japonica 'Halliana'

MILDEW

Honeysuckles (*Lonicera*) are especially prone to the fungal infection known as mildew because they are often planted in unsuitable hot, sunny sites. Dry roots and a still atmosphere are triggers for the disease. There are two kinds of mildew, downy and powdery. Both appear as a white powdery coating on the leaves. With downy mildew this is on the underside; with powdery mildew it is on the upper surface.

Treatment involves spraying with a systemic fungicide; although this will not cure the existing problem, it will prevent further infection. It is best to cut out the infected parts of the plant, or at least remove and destroy the affected foliage.

Watering the ground well in dry weather helps to discourage mildew and a preventative spray with a systemic fungicide in spring and summer is useful for previously infected plants.

---

species. **'Hall's Prolific'** is a selection from 'Halliana' that blooms profusely even when very young and has larger flowers (see Good Companions, below left). It does, however, seem to be more prone to mildew than 'Halliana'.

The young leaves of *Lonicera japonica* are often completely different from the adult foliage, with deep, rounded lobes. The leaves of **'Horwood Gem'** are especially deeply lobed and have a rich cream and apricot-pink flush, which gives a really lush appearance.

Parthenocissus (see pages 146–47) are the classic choice for a high wall. These vines are often collectively known as Virginia creepers, but strictly this name belongs only to the species *Parthenocissus quinquefolia*. Parthenocissus are self-clinging and spread themselves evenly across walls, reaching a height of 15m (50ft). The flowers are insignificant but are sometimes followed by small, blue-black fruit. The leaves are usually plain green and deeply divided. In autumn, they change to blazing orange and flaming red shades before falling.

Parthenocissus are easy to get established and the only maintenance they need is an annual or biennial trim as the cover gets thicker to stop the weight of the growth, or strong winds, pulling them away from the wall.

GOOD COMPANIONS

Clematis VINO ('Poulvo') (1) has delicious deep wine flowers that follow on from the deep purple flowers of the chocolate vine, *Akebia quinata* (2).

Lonicera japonica 'Hall's Prolific' and *Clematis montana* var. *rubens* (3) have complementary flowering times: the honeysuckle takes over in early summer, when the clematis has finished.

Hedera colchica 'Dentata Variegata'♔ (4) can be livened up with the nodding flowers of the viticella hybrid *Clematis* 'Minuet'♔ (5), borne from midsummer onwards.

Pyrostegia venusta • *Rosa filipes* 'Kiftsgate' • *Rosa* 'Rambling Rector' • *Vitis coignetiae* • *Wisteria floribunda* •

Sheltered gardens

A surprising number of gardens have a microclimate that enables more tender climbing plants to be grown outdoors. The warm western coastal areas of Britain are well known for their lush gardens, and some inland areas have the same conditions – perhaps the result of a sheltered valley or walled garden. In the USA the southern states have similar or yet more favourable growing conditions, and some gardeners are fortunate enough to be able to grow conservatory plants outside.

Abelia floribunda

Like a walled or a valley garden, an area that is sheltered by a belt of trees – such as this sunny hillside at Hadspen Garden, in Somerset – is the perfect environment for climbers that need some protection from cold temperatures.

Sometimes having a sheltered site is something of a headache. Finding out exactly how sheltered it is can be difficult; the best advice is to be bold and test the boundaries. Often you can grow very tender plants quite happily. They may get killed in an exceptional winter, but new plants will quickly grow again and fill the space.

Given the shelter of a warm wall, **Abelia floribunda**♥ is a relatively safe choice. In early summer, it has brilliant pink, pendulous, tubular flowers, much longer and more vibrant than in the more shrubby abelias; each bloom is backed with characteristic dull red sepals. A native of Mexico, it has evergreen, glossy green foliage and its slender, arching growth reaches 3m (10ft).

There is a very wide range of abutilons, some of which are hardier than others (see also page 38). **Abutilon 'Canary Bird'**♥ is a superb shrub for a sheltered wall. It has glossy green, evergreen foliage and grows to 3m (10ft). The large, bell-shaped, lemon-yellow flowers appear from early summer to late autumn. Another good hybrid is **Abutilon 'Kentish Belle'**♥, which is semi-evergreen with purplish stems and long, pointed, dark green leaves. The flowers are rich apricot with a hint of red in the veins and are produced all through summer and autumn. It is low-growing,

EVERGREEN CLIMBERS AND WALL SHRUBS FOR SHELTERED SITES *Acacia baileyana* 'Purpurea' •

Abutilon 'Kentish Belle'

Abutilon megapotamicum

Billardiera longiflora 'Cherry Berry'

Abutilon 'Canary Bird'

Abutilon vitifolium 'Veronica Tennant'

Billardiera longiflora

to 1.2m (4ft), and so is an ideal choice for planting against a low wall. (See Good Companions, page 57.)

Abutilon megapotamicum♛ is a graceful, lax wall shrub, with semi-evergreen, rich green foliage. Trained onto a wall the plant will reach 2m (6ft) and produce masses of pendulous, yellow flowers with very prominent red sepals. These are borne from mid-spring until late autumn and give a wonderful exotic feel to a planting scheme without being too greedy for space. *Abutilon megapotamicum* 'Variegatum' is an excellent variegated form with a wonderful gold-mottled leaf.

Abutilon vitifolium 'Veronica Tennant'♛ is a much larger and lusher plant. It is a soft-wooded, short-lived wall shrub, growing to 3m (10ft). The large,

hollyhock-like flowers, produced very freely from mid-spring to midsummer, are a delicate shade of mauve and look gorgeous with the soft grey, deciduous foliage. It is the ideal choice for a sheltered site in the angle of two walls.

Billardiera longiflora is an amazing evergreen, twining climber from Australia. It has long, pendulous, bell-shaped, greenish-yellow flowers in early summer, but it is grown more for the brilliant deep purple fruit that follow the flowers in early autumn. There are also forms with reddish or white fruit, but the purple is by far the most striking. It has a large underground tuber and so will cope with a really dry spot. It also makes excellent ground cover in dry areas. It needs shelter from cold winds and strong sun. Its maximum height is 3m (10ft).

For an elegant, deciduous wall shrub in a sheltered spot, *Buddleja crispa* is hard to beat. This gorgeous felty-leaved plant grows to 3m (10ft) and produces 12cm (5in) long panicles of tangerine-throated,

Buddleja crispa

55

Ceanothus arboreus 'Trewithen Blue'

Clematis florida var. flore-pleno

Clematis florida PISTACHIO

Clematis florida var. sieboldiana

lilac flowers from early summer right through to the first frosts. Like all buddleias, it flowers as it grows, so is best cut back hard in spring. On a wall this means building up a framework of branches to prune to.

If you have a large space consider the self-clinging, deciduous climber **Campsis grandiflora**, growing to 6m (20ft). This is one of the parents of *Campsis* × *tagliabuana* 'Madame Galen'♀ (see page 39). One of the most beautiful of all the campsis, it is also one of the least hardy. Drooping panicles of rich, deep orange-red flowers are produced in late summer and early autumn, on the current season's growth. It must have full sun to ripen the growth sufficiently to bear flowers.

One of the most gorgeous of all the **ceanothus** is the lovely, tender, large-leaved, evergreen **Ceanothus arboreus 'Trewithen Blue'**♀. It has a loose-limbed elegance, making it just as classy a wall shrub as, for example, *Magnolia grandiflora* (see page 40) or *Camellia japonica* (see page 117). Reaching a height of 6m (20ft), it has large panicles of lightly scented, blue flowers in spring and early summer. (See Good Companions, right.)

Clematis florida is one of the main parents of today's large-flowered, deciduous hybrid clematis, but the species itself has been lost in cultivation and may no longer exist in the wild, having been cross-pollinated by cultivated hybrids. Some selections have been made in clematis nurseries, but how close they are to the true species is not yet known. One that is now available is **Clematis florida** PISTACHIO **('Evirida')**. From early summer to early autumn this has creamy-white flowers with deep purple anthers and a bright green clump of malformed styles in the centre. The later flowers take on a greenish flush. Although it is reported to be very free-flowering and reaches 3m (10ft), it seems to be a weak grower, and will need to rely on neighbouring plants for support.

A much better choice is the idiosyncratic **Clematis florida var. sieboldiana** ('Sieboldii'). It has creamy-white flowers, 10cm (4in) across, each with a mass of purple petal-like stamens in the centre, making it resemble a passion flower. (See Good Companions, right, and see page 74.) It grows to 3m (10ft) and flowers continuously from early summer to early autumn. Given a warm wall it will flower very freely, the central boss of stamens remaining long after the creamy sepals have dropped. However, to say that it is unstable would be an understatement. In some years, it may revert to an all-white, fully double form, known as **Clematis florida var. flore-pleno** ('Alba Plena'), or it may even produce half and half blooms, where half of the flower is true *Clematis*

MORE CLIMBERS AND WALL SHRUBS FOR SHELTERED SITES *Albizia julibrissin* • *Aloysia triphylla* •

Coronilla valentina subsp. glauca 'Variegata'

Rosa banksiae 'Lutea'

Rosa 'Mermaid'

florida var. *sieboldiana* (creamy white and single, with purple stamens), the other *Clematis florida* var. *flore-pleno* (all white and fully double).

For a low wall **Coronilla valentina subsp. glauca 'Citrina'**♥ is delightful. This evergreen shrub grows to just 1.5m (5ft) and produces masses of pale yellow, pea-like flowers, with a sweet scent, from late winter to early spring and again in late summer. **Coronilla valentina subsp. glauca 'Variegata'** is equally good, with cool creamy-white variegation in the leaves and richer yellow flowers.

One of the loveliest plants for a sheltered site is **Rosa banksiae 'Lutea'**♥, the Banksian rose. It is a loose-growing, arching climber with light green, semi-evergreen leaves on almost thornless stems. It has the most delightful clusters of tiny yellow flowers, produced in great profusion in mid- or late spring. Their flowering coincides with that of wisteria, and the two make a perfect partnership when grown together (see pages 98–99). The rose is vigorous, reaching a height of 7.5m (25ft) or more, and loves a warm, sunny wall to help the wood ripen and produce flower buds.

Another rose that needs a sheltered wall is **Rosa 'Mermaid'**♥. This gorgeous semi-evergreen climber, up to 6m (20ft) tall, has large, single, sulphur-yellow flowers, up to 15cm (6in) across, with deep amber stamens that hold their colour even after the petals have dropped. The foliage is a glossy green and is freely produced, giving the rose a lush appearance.

GOOD COMPANIONS

Cistus × *pulverulentus* 'Sunset'♥ (1) planted at the foot of *Abutilon* 'Kentish Belle'♥ (2) will hide the abutilon's slightly skinny base.

Ceanothus arboreus 'Trewithen Blue'♥ (3) finishes flowering by early summer, so using it as a host for *Clematis* 'Princess Diana'♥ (4) makes good use of the open branches in late summer.

Clematis florida var. *sieboldiana* (5) needs a host with strong branches, such as *Chaenomeles speciosa* 'Yukigoten' (6), to support its weak stems.

57

Callistemon citrinus • *Citrus* × *meyeri* 'Meyer' • *Muehlenbeckia complexa* • *Wisteria brachybotrys* 'Shiro-kapitan' •

Conservatories

A conservatory or sun room allows you to bring the garden right into the home, which is a real boon – for both people and plants – especially in cold, wet winters. It also offers the chance to grow some of the more exotic climbers, many of which can be moved outside when the weather warms up.

Conservatories used to be reserved for growing plants, but today they often double up as a living space, so climbers need to look good even when out of flower. The glossy green leaves of *Camellia reticulata* 'Captain Rawes' are attractive throughout the year, even without the silky, rose-pink flowers.

A conservatory can be a difficult growing environment, with high light levels and extreme temperatures. This means that, without some intervention, only a very few plants will survive. Adding blinds or even a leafy climber and, ideally, automatic ventilation will ensure that your climbers do not suffer through drought or high temperatures and that they grow and flower freely. They will also be much more resistant to the ever-present conservatory pests and diseases. Finally, be sure to use a large enough pot and a quality soil-based compost (see page 79).

Alyogyne huegelii 'Santa Cruz'

Alyogyne huegelii 'Santa Cruz' is an exotic evergreen wall shrub that loves a baking hot spot and needs the frost protection afforded by a conservatory in winter. It quickly attains its mature

WINTER HEAT LOSS

During the winter, conservatory temperatures can dip dangerously low at night, despite the warmth of the house's central heating. This is particularly serious and damaging for young plants, which are not as tolerant of low temperatures as more mature specimens.

Methods such as lining the roof or windows with the bubble insulation used in greenhouses are not an option in conservatories. Light levels will already be poorer than in a greenhouse and aesthetics are a prime concern. Reducing the amount of water you give in these cold months, when plants are not flowering, is the best way of preventing damage. •

MORE GOOD CLIMBERS AND WALL PLANTS FOR CONSERVATORIES *Allamanda cathartica* 'Hendersonii' •

height of 3m (10ft) and bears rich, satiny mauve, funnel-shaped flowers all through the summer, scattered among the large, palmate, green leaves. It is rather short-lived, and it is worth taking a few cuttings each year so that you have a replacement plant ready to take over.

Bougainvillea glabra♔ and its hybrids are a familiar sight in Mediterranean countries and in the southern USA. Bougainvilleas take the place of roses in hot climates, providing vibrant colour from late spring to early summer; in very warm years, they then flower again from early autumn until early winter. Each bloom consists of a cluster of vivid purple, petal-like bracts surrounding three small tubular, creamy-white flowers. The dark green leaves are an ovate shape that is echoed in the bracts.

In the wild in Brazil, *Bougainvillea glabra* stretches its thorny, evergreen

Bougainvillea × buttiana

Bougainvillea glabra

Bougainvillea glabra 'Sanderiana'

Bougainvillea 'Alexandra'

MOVING PLANTS OUTDOORS

Conservatory plants enjoy sunning themselves on the patio in summer. It freshens up the foliage, helps to ripen the wood and discourages pests. Timing is vital: don't take plants outside until all danger of frost is past, and bring them back in as soon as the weather starts to cool.

Only climbers on free-standing supports can be treated this way, so when you plant a climber consider whether you may want to move it outside later, and provide a suitable support. Bamboo is a good material, being light but very strong; large fan shapes and double hoops are ideal. Metal supports get very hot in conservatories and can cause damage to plants growing on them.

Pot stands with castors are useful for moving plants around, but muscle power is still needed to negotiate sills and changes in levels. Never try moving large, heavy pots on your own.

stems over trees to reach 10m (33ft) or more; growing it in a pot will restrict its height to 4m (13ft). *Bougainvillea glabra* 'Sanderiana' is a loose-limbed, purple form that resembles the species. It needs a regular minimum temperature of 10°C (50°F) to thrive, but may survive very short spells at 0°C (32°F).

The species *Bougainvillea glabra* has been crossed with *Bougainvillea peruviana* to create the stunning *Bougainvillea × buttiana*. It comes in a wide range of bright colours from pink through purple, orange, apricot and yellow to cream. These highly coloured hybrids are less hardy and more temperamental than forms of *Bougainvillea glabra*. Very often they are sold unnamed, but it is worth hunting out some of the best varieties. *Bougainvillea* 'Alexandra' is rich, vivid

purple (see Good Companions, page 61); *Bougainvillea × buttiana* 'Mrs Butt'♔, sometimes incorrectly known as *Bougainvillea* 'Crimson Lake', is a stunning magenta colour flushed with crimson; and *Bougainvillea* 'Dania' is a bold cerise-pink.

Camellia reticulata is an evergreen, tender species, with glossy, dark green leaves, that is rather rare in gardens. The wavy-petalled, rose-red flowers, produced in early and mid-spring, are much larger than those of *Camellia japonica* (see page 117), but the plant's lack of hardiness has kept it scarce. *Camellia reticulata* 'Captain Rawes' is one of the most beautiful forms, with semi-double, ruffled, dark rose-pink blooms, 12cm (5in) wide. *Camellia reticulata* 'Mary Williams' has single, rich rose-pink flowers of the same

Beaumontia grandiflora • Bomarea caldasii • Clerodendrum thomsoniae • Gloriosa superba 'Rothschildiana' •

Hardenbergia violacea

Jasminum polyanthum

Hoya carnosa

Lapageria rosea

rose on the outside and are produced in numerous panicles from late winter through to late summer, against rich green, pinnate leaves. It is vigorous and will easily reach up to 4m (13ft), more if it is well cared for, but it can be pruned after flowering to keep it in check. (See Good Companions, right.)

If space is more limited *Jasminum sambac*♀ (Arabian jasmine), another evergreen twiner, growing to just 3m (10ft), is a good choice. The mid-green leaves are reduced to only one leaflet

size. In the wild these shrubs reach up to 15m (50ft), but 4m (13ft) is more usual when grown in a pot in a conservatory.

For a conservatory that mainly catches the sun in the afternoon, *Hardenbergia violacea*♀ (purple coral pea), from Australia, is a stunning choice. An evergreen, twining climber, it prefers protection from the hottest sun but still likes plenty of light. The pea-like, lavender flowers are carried in hanging racemes over slender, lance-shaped, glossy green leaves, from late winter to early summer. This long flowering period combined with a compact habit of 2m (6ft) makes it ideal for small conservatories.

In the wild, *Hoya carnosa*♀ (wax plant) is often epiphytic, living in trees in the rainforest. The clusters of fleshy,

white flowers, borne from late spring to autumn, have rusty-red centres and are night-scented to attract pollinating insects. The evergreen leaves are thick, oval and waxy-looking. A self-clinging climber, using aerial roots to help it clamber upwards, it grows to 6m (20ft) with the support of a trellis. It needs some protection from the brightest sunlight.

The more exotic species of **jasmine** are fabulous for the conservatory. *Jasminum polyanthum*♀, an evergreen, twining climber, is familiar to us as a houseplant, trained on circular hoops, but this treatment does not make the best of its gorgeous, intensely fragrant flowers. Letting it reach its full potential in a conservatory unleashes an elegant beauty. The white flowers are flushed

CONSERVATORY PESTS

Scale insects and red spider mites are two of the commonest pests affecting plants grown in a conservatory.

Small, brown or white, shell-like patches on the undersides of leaves and on stems are a sign of scale insects. Sooty mould, a black sooty layer on the leaves, can also be a sign of an advanced attack, since this grows on the sugary honeydew that scale insects exude. The insects live beneath the 'scales' and suck the sap from the plant. Treatment is with a systemic insecticide; a long-acting form will help prevent reinfestation.

The dry atmosphere often found in conservatories is the perfect breeding ground for red spider mites. These tiny mites suck the sap from plants, causing a distinctive fine mottling of the leaves; in advanced cases, a fine webbing will be seen. Close inspection will reveal tiny crawling insects that turn red in autumn.

Spraying with insecticide is effective but must be repeated exactly as directed to ensure all generations are killed. Biological control is also very effective but needs warm temperatures for the predatory mites to survive and feed. Misting will help create a more humid atmosphere, which discourages red spider mites.

MORE GOOD CLIMBERS AND WALL PLANTS FOR CONSERVATORIES *Mutisia decurrens • Nerium oleander •*

and are carried on more angular stems. The clusters of large white flowers have a heavy fragrance and are produced primarily in summer, but also intermittently throughout the year.

Another climber that needs shade or semi-shade is **Lapageria rosea**♀; more often than not this fails because it is grown in strong sunlight. The long, bell-shaped, fleshy, rose-pink flowers are very showy and are carried through summer and autumn on strong, twining stems, with dark green, grooved, ovate leaves. Reaching a height of 5m (16ft), it needs a lime-free soil or ericaceous compost. A mulch with slate or gravel will help keep the compost cool and moist.

Passion flowers (see page 141) are evergreen, tendril climbers, most of which need the protection that a conservatory provides. **Passiflora × violacea**♀ has rich purple-red flowers from summer through to autumn. The leaves are five-lobed and carried on very vigorous growth.

Passiflora × violacea

This species is suitable only for larger conservatories, as it will easily reach 5m (16ft) and very likely considerably more.

Sollya heterophylla♀, the bluebell climber (see also page 113), is a perfect candidate for a conservatory, with clusters of nodding, sky-blue flowers borne on twining stems of small, evergreen foliage. Less well known are the pink and white forms, **Sollya heterophylla** 'Pink

Sollya heterophylla

Stephanotis floribunda

Charmer' and **Sollya heterophylla** 'Alba'. All three flower throughout summer and autumn. This extended flowering period curbs the plant's growth and it reaches just 2m (6ft), making it ideal for a restricted space.

The Madagascar jasmine, **Stephanotis floribunda**♀, is a gorgeous plant. The white, waxy, star-shaped flowers are highly perfumed and are produced from spring to autumn, among glossy, ovate, evergreen leaves. A twining climber, the plant will eventually reach 5m (16ft) but takes some time to do so. To thrive, it needs a humus-rich, well-drained compost, a steady temperature and a position in semi-shade in summer, otherwise it will succumb to insect attack. (See Good Companions, left.)

GOOD COMPANIONS

Plumbago auriculata (1) begins flowering in late summer, just as *Jasminum polyanthum* (2) starts to falter. The plumbago can be cut back as the jasmine is about to flower again in late winter.

Bougainvillea 'Alexandra' (3) planted with the annual *Ipomoea lobata* (4) creates a wonderful exotic feel. An added bonus is that the ipomoea foliage makes up for the sparseness of the bougainvillea leaves.

Use × *Fatshedera lizei* 'Variegata'♀ (5) to conceal the bare stems of *Stephanotis floribunda*♀ (6); also, the cream variegation in the fatshedera foliage will pick out the flower colour of the stephanotis.

Passiflora 'Amethyst' • *Passiflora quadrangularis* • *Pyrostegia venusta* • *Streptosolen jamesonii* • *Tecoma capensis* •

Garden features

Increasingly climbers are moving away from walls and fences and finding their way into the garden proper, supported on all manner of free-standing structures such as arches, arbours, pergolas and obelisks. Thoughtfully placed and imaginatively planted, such features can create a focal point, frame a view, divide one area of the garden from another, enclose a walkway, or enhance a seating area.

The key factor when planning a garden feature is balance: your aim is to enhance both the feature and the climber by putting them together. An obelisk completely lost under a vigorous climber is contributing nothing to the garden design; you might as well use a trio of bamboo canes. On the other hand, something as large as a pergola will look woefully underdressed with just one or two lightly foliaged plants struggling to cover its pillars.

Rosa 'American Pillar' is a large, rambling rose suitable for training over really wide structures, such as these elegant metal arches in Monet's garden at Giverny, France.

Early large-flowered **clematis** hybrids, growing to 2.5–3m (8–10ft), are extremely good for garden features. Often used alongside other climbers, they tend to have very delicate stems that appreciate the extra support. The usual flowering period is from late spring to early summer

PLACING ARCHES, ARBOURS, PERGOLAS AND OBELISKS

So often, arches are set in the middle of the lawn, straddling the path – not the most dramatic or even useful placing. Arches are really good at creating the illusion of space. Long, thin gardens are improved by putting an arch towards the rear of the garden off the centre line. Make sure that another feature such as a statue or a striking plant is visible beyond the arch to draw the eye.

Arbours tend to suffer a similar fate, being placed at the end of a path facing back towards the house. It would be much better to have the arbour facing a focal point in the garden or so that it catches the early morning or late evening sunshine and provides a special spot to sit in. Choose climbers with scented flowers for seating areas and plant aromatic shrubs at the base to shield their roots and provide fragrance when the climbers are not in bloom.

Pergolas can be used in many different ways. They are superb at dividing garden areas, their bulk creating a natural division without completely blocking the view. Sited close to the house they act as a link between living space and garden. Choose a generously proportioned pergola as it will allow two people to walk side by side beneath it. An imaginatively planned pergola can also double up as a seating area or dining space, shaded from the heat of the sun.

Obelisks are especially useful in small gardens, lending height at any point without taking up space. The trick to siting an obelisk is to place it well forward in the border. This stops it from simply blending into the planting; it makes a stronger statement and it also allows the climbers it supports to be seen at closer quarters.

GOOD ANNUAL CLIMBERS FOR GARDEN FEATURES *Cobaea scandens* • *Ipomoea tricolor* 'Heavenly Blue' •

CLEMATIS WILT

Many clematis lovers live in dread of clematis wilt, a fungal disease that perhaps more correctly should be called stem rot. The fungus enters the plant primarily through the leaves, spreading down through the leaf-stalk into the stem. Infected tissue turns a jet black colour, easily identified when dry and powdery, and because no sap can pass through this area, the stem above it wilts, turns brown and dies.

The fungus can also enter through wounds caused by insects and by bent stems, but infection of this kind can generally be prevented by careful cultivation.

Some varieties are resistant to the infection, but others, and especially the beautiful early large-flowered hybrids, are particularly susceptible to it, a factor thought to be genetic.

Protection is all but impossible in the garden. The only sure solution for now is to avoid susceptible varieties, but this would deprive us of some of our best-loved clematis. The most useful technique is deep planting (see page 29); burying no more than 8cm (3in) of stem underground will allow new shoots to form should the variety be affected by wilt. The future does look brighter: new chemicals are heading onto the market and our much better understanding of the problem should help us to prevent the disease in time.

The following clematis species are resistant to wilt:

Clematis alpina⚘
Clematis armandii
Clematis cirrhosa
Clematis koreana
Clematis macropetala
Clematis montana
Clematis texensis
Clematis tibetana subsp. *vernayi*
Clematis viticella⚘

Clematis 'Lady Northcliffe'

Clematis 'Multi Blue'

Clematis 'Lasurstern'

and again in late summer. They will either give double flower power if chosen to coincide with the other climber, or extend the season if flowering at a different time. Roses are generally the partner of choice, but clematis combine happily with all but the weakest-growing climbers.

These early large-flowered hybrids are some of the most spectacular clematis, but sadly they are also the most susceptible to clematis wilt (see box).

Clematis 'Kathleen Wheeler' has huge, reddish-purple flowers, 23cm (9in) across, with golden anthers and lilac filaments, borne in late spring and early summer with more in late summer and early autumn. Being so large, the flowers need shelter from damaging winds.

Clematis 'King Edward VII' is a compact plant with 15cm (6in) wide, lilac-mauve flowers, a contrasting pink central bar and brown anthers. It is a good choice for confined areas but, as with most striped hybrids (see pages 42–43), it keeps its bright colouring best in shade.

Clematis 'Lady Northcliffe' has rich violet-blue, wavy flowers, 12cm (5in)

wide, with black-tipped, creamy stamens. It has a very long period of flower from early summer through to early autumn and often longer if the weather is warm.

A real old favourite and still very highly regarded is *Clematis* 'Lasurstern'⚘. It has large, lavender-blue flowers, 18cm (7in) wide, with creamy-yellow anthers. As with many blue clematis, the flowers are almost iridescent, with hints of other colours within the sepals.

Another excellent hybrid is *Clematis* 'Louise Rowe'. It has a wonderful mix of single, semi-double and double flowers all at the same time. These are 15cm (6in) across with broad, rounded, overlapping sepals in a delicate shade of pale lilac with creamy anthers.

Clematis 'Multi Blue' is a stunning, but slightly unstable, sport of 'The President'⚘ (see page 80). It has large, double, blue flowers, 15cm (6in) across, with a mass of petal-like stamens. These last long after the sepals have dropped, making it an excellent choice for a small space. The flowers are borne from early summer through to early autumn. There are several strains, producing flowers with varying numbers of petals; it is best to buy the plant in bloom so that you can see exactly what you are getting.

One of the first large-flowered hybrids to bloom is *Clematis* 'Sir Garnet Wolseley'; it gives a lovely early show, with the later blooms being a little sporadic. The flowers are mauve with red anthers and are 15cm (6in) wide. They have a slight scent of violets.

63

Lathyrus odoratus 'Matucana' • *Phaseolus coccineus* • *Thunbergia alata* • *Tropaeolum majus* •

Rosa A SHROPSHIRE LAD

Rosa CONSTANCE SPRY

Rosa FALSTAFF

Rosa CROWN PRINCESS MARGARETA

Rosa GERTRUDE JEKYLL

Roses are excellent for garden features, combining beautifully with clematis to make stunning focal points. When choosing, look for good repeat flowering, a neat habit of growth and, ideally, rich fragrance. David Austin's English roses fit this bill perfectly. This group of roses combines the bushy habit, flower form and fragrance of the old shrub roses with the repeat-flowering qualities and wider colour range of modern varieties. They are strong, healthy growers, and blend attractively with shrubs and herbaceous plants. Some of the taller varieties also make extremely successful climbers. When grown like this they generally reach around 2.5–3m (8–10ft) and flower from late spring to mid-autumn.

Rosa A SHROPSHIRE LAD ('Ausled') is one of the few true climbers in this group. It is ideal for garden features, being nearly thornless and very sweetly scented. The flowers are soft peachy pink and form lovely cupped rosettes.

GOOD COMPANIONS

Clematis cirrhosa var. *balearica* (1) provides valuable winter flowers when *Rosa* FALSTAFF ('Ausverse') (2) is dormant, as well as a good green foliage contrast when the rose is in full bloom.

Plant *Rosa* A SHROPSHIRE LAD ('Ausled') (3) with *Clematis macropetala* 'Wesselton' (4) to create a quintessential English look. The rose offers excellent physical support to the clematis.

Rosa SPIRIT OF FREEDOM ('Ausbite') (5) and old-fashioned sweet peas (*Lathyrus odoratus*) (6) give a long flowering season and fill the air with scent.

MORE GOOD CLIMBERS AND WALL SHRUBS FOR GARDEN FEATURES *Abutilon megapotamicum* •

Rosa CONSTANCE SPRY ('Ausfirst')♀ is unusual in the English roses in having only one flush of flower, but the luminous clear pink blooms are exquisite. It grows to 4m (13ft) and looks superb on a large pergola or on a house wall (see page 24).

Rosa CROWN PRINCESS MARGARETA ('Auswinter') is one of the shrubs suitable for growing as a climber. The flowers are a fabulous shade of glowing apricot-orange. Strong and healthy, it is an excellent first rose to try.

Rosa FALSTAFF ('Ausverse') is a rich, dark crimson, and makes a wonderful contrast with light-coloured clematis. A healthy grower that doesn't get too big, it is ideal on an obelisk. (See Good Companions, below left.)

Rosa GERTRUDE JEKYLL ('Ausbord')♀ is probably the best rose in this group. The slightly flattened, rich pink flowers are profusely borne all summer long. Their fragrance is unrivalled, and considered so good that this was the first rose used to make rose essence in Britain in 250 years.

Rosa SPIRIT OF FREEDOM ('Ausbite') has a strong myrrh fragrance and large, deeply cupped, clear pink flowers. Smaller than some varieties, it is good for obelisks and pergola posts.

OTHER GOOD FLOWERING CLIMBERS FOR GARDEN FEATURES

Dregea sinensis (**1**) is evergreen, with ovate leaves, grey beneath, and white, scented flowers in summer. A fairly formal-looking plant, very useful on metal arches. Height 3m (10ft).

Lonicera periclymenum 'Graham Thomas'♀ (**2**) has deciduous, green leaves, and richly scented, creamy-yellow flowers all summer. Full of rustic charm, and delightful for an arbour. Height 7m (22ft).

Passiflora caerulea 'White Lightning' (see page 141) is an evergreen, with blue-green leaves and intricate white flowers from late spring to the frosts. A slender plant, excellent where width is limited. Trouble free. Height 8m (26ft).

Rhodochiton atrosanguineus♀ (see page 108) is herbaceous, with green, heart-shaped leaves, and purple, tubular, bell-shaped flowers all summer long. Hard to find but worth the hunt if you have an exotic planting scheme. Height 3m (10ft).

Sollya heterophylla♀ (see page 113) has evergreen, small green leaves, and blue, bell-like flowers in clusters in summer and autumn. A neat grower suited to an arch or obelisk in a sheltered garden. Height 2m (6ft).

Trachelospermum jasminoides♀ (see page 96) has evergreen, glossy green, oval leaves, and starry, white, richly scented flowers all summer. Excellent on a pergola. Height 7m (22ft).

GOOD FOLIAGE CLIMBERS FOR GARDEN FEATURES

Actinidia pilosula (see page 116) is a slender and striking climber, ideal for an obelisk. It has deciduous, elegant, narrow leaves, the tips dipped white, and pink flowers in spring. Height 3m (10ft).

Ampelopsis brevipedunculata var. *maximowiczii* 'Elegans' (see page 39) has deciduous, small, vine-shaped leaves in green, white and pink. Brightly coloured and compact, good in small spaces. Height 3m (10ft).

Hedera helix 'Goldchild'♀ (see page 101) has evergreen leaves variegated creamy gold. Height 1.2m (4ft).

Humulus lupulus 'Aureus'♀ (**1**), the golden hop (see page 102), is a herbaceous climber with bright golden leaves and hop flowers in mid- to late summer. Height 6m (20ft): will cover a pergola with ease and can be used on smaller features if trimmed.

Jasminum officinale FIONA SUNRISE ('Frojas') (see pages 49 and 103) has deciduous, rich golden yellow, pinnate foliage, and a light crop of scented, starry, white flowers in summer. Height 2–4m (6–13ft). Combines refined habit with stunning colour, ideal for smaller features.

Lonicera japonica 'Mint Crisp' (**2**) is semi-evergreen, with creamy-mottled leaves and creamy-yellow, richly scented summer flowers. Has a cooling effect on colour schemes. Gorgeous with soft lemon climbing roses. Height 6m (20ft).

65

Planting through shrubs and trees

Shrubs and trees make excellent settings for climbers, showing off their flowers and fruit to perfection. In return, the climbing plants perform any of a number of services: breaking up an expanse of bare trunk, adding highlights to a dense green canopy, or bringing a second season of interest to a shrub once its own flowering period is over.

Acer platanoides 'Drummondii'

is an effective host for smaller blue and purple climbers, while *Acer platanoides* 'Drummondii' is good for larger ones. If your climber has small dainty flowers, try using a tree or shrub with big bold leaves to stop the design looking too busy: the large-leaved *Aucuba japonica* (spotted laurel) is useful for foliage contrast, as is *Magnolia* × *soulangeana*, which has the special bonus of large, deep reddish-pink to white flowers in spring.

Clematis montana 'Alexander' showers gracefully through the Persian ivy, *Hedera colchica*.

Growing two plants together in this way demands careful planning, to make sure that neither host nor guest will swamp its partner. Where the host is a slow grower give it a few years' head start. When choosing planting partners, consider the pruning requirements of both plants: it is essential that they don't conflict otherwise you may lose the flowers on your climber. Think about combinations of flower colour and shape, as well as foliage size and shape. Blue and purple flowers tend to be recessive and need a bright background to show them off: the cream-variegated dogwood *Cornus alba* 'Elegantissima'♥

Cornus alba 'Elegantissima'

Magnolia × soulangeana 'Rustica Rubra'

PLANTING CLIMBERS THROUGH SHRUBS

Planting through established shrubs gives the best results. Always plant the rootball on the shady side of the shrub; this encourages the climber to wind its way across to the sunny side.

Dig a generous planting hole under the shrub canopy, and improve the soil with organic matter. Keep well watered until the climber has become established.

Many clematis have light foliage that sits well among other plants, and there is a seemingly infinite choice, with species and hybrids of every level of vigour, flowering time and colour. *Clematis* 'Arabella'♡ is often recommended for growing through shrubs but it is a magnet for mildew. Most gardens will do far better with the lovely hybrid *Clematis* 'Alionushka'♡ (**1**). This is a non-clinging clematis but reaches an easy 2m (6ft), making it ideal for threading through shrubs. It has pink, hanging, bell-shaped flowers, with upturned tips, from early summer to early autumn. Large, loose-limbed shrubs such as the dramatic, silver-leaved *Elaeagnus* 'Quicksilver'♡ (**2**) or the spring-flowering, deep purple, richly scented lilac, *Syringa vulgaris* 'Charles Joly'♡ (**3**) make excellent hosts.

Clematis 'Huldine'♡ (**1**) is an unusual hybrid with translucent, pearly-white flowers that have a mauve stripe along the back of the sepals. It grows to 6m (20ft) and flowers from late summer to late autumn. It looks stunning growing through a tall, evergreen shrub, for example the spring-flowering *Ceanothus* 'Concha'♡ (**2**) (see page 111), where the underside of the clematis flower can be seen at close quarters. Both the clematis and the ceanothus require sun to thrive.

The deep purple *Clematis* 'Jackmanii'♡ was the first of the true large-flowered hybrids and is still extremely popular. Sadly, it does have a tendency to clematis wilt, possibly introduced through one of its parents, *Clematis lanuginosa* (see page 10). The hybrid *Clematis* 'Gipsy Queen'♡ (**1**) has very similar colouring but different parentage and is a better choice (see page 105). *Philadelphus* 'Virginal' (**2**), the very richly scented, double mock orange, makes a charming companion, bursting into blossom at midsummer, right in the middle of 'Gipsy Queen's' long flowering period. Both reach a height of 3m (10ft).

Clematis montana is a fabulous, strong-growing, deciduous climber, reaching a height of 8m (26ft), and is ideal for growing through other, equally vigorous plants. It flowers profusely from late spring to early summer. In the species the flowers are white, but the pink varieties, such as Clematis montana var. rubens 'Pink Perfection' (**1**), are probably better known. (See also page 123.)

The larger Japanese flowering cherries, for example Prunus 'Kanzan'♀ and Prunus 'Taihaku'♀ (**2**), make lovely partners for Clematis montana cultivars, the clematis flowers opening just as the cherries finish. They are especially good in wet springs, when the cherry blossom gets knocked off prematurely by rain. Large ornamental crab apples, for example Malus 'Directeur Moerlands' (**3**), and birch, such as Betula pendula 'Purpurea', are also good hosts. Think about colour combinations when choosing: pink montana blossom can get completely lost on a pink-flowered malus, and a white variety may be a better choice.

Clematis montana 'Alexander' (see page 66) is a selection of the white species, with much larger leaves and flowers. The slower-growing Clematis 'Marjorie' (**4**) has semi-double, soft pink flowers with salmon-pink centres. Both need a sunny spot.

Clematis 'Mayleen'♀ (**5**) is one of the best scented montanas, with a delicate, slightly elusive aroma of vanilla or almonds. The flowers are satin pink, the young foliage is bronze and the plant grows to a height of 10m (33ft). If growing it through a blossom tree then choose one with a contrasting foliage colour, such as the silver Sorbus thibetica 'John Mitchell'♀ (**6**); alternatively grow it through a tree with deep plum foliage, for example the bold-leaved Acer platanoides 'Crimson King'♀ (**7**), for dramatic effect.

MORE CLIMBERS FOR GROWING THROUGH SHRUBS AND TREES Clematis florida var. sieboldiana •

Clematis 'Ville de Lyon' (**1**) has very lovely carmine-red flowers with even darker margins and golden stamens; it flowers very freely and reaches a height of 3m (10ft). It is best known, however, for a tendency to have dead foliage at its base. This is not caused by poor cultivation: the oldest foliage on the lower part of the plant always turns brown and dies. The simple solution is to plant it through a medium-sized shrub such as the pink and plum variegated *Berberis thunbergii* f. *atropurpurea* 'Harlequin' (**2**): the dead clematis foliage will be hidden and the stunning flowers take centre stage.

Clematis viticella♀ and its hybrids (see page 139) are ideal climbers for growing through shrubs. They are all pruned hard in winter, which allows the untidy dead growth to be pulled out, leaving the host shrub to give a solo performance until the new clematis growth begins in spring. *Clematis* 'Minuet'♀ (**1**) has purple and white flowers that contrast beautifully with the lime green of *Itea ilicifolia*♀ (**2**) – an evergreen, summer-flowering wall shrub with long green tassels (see page 137). The clematis grows to 3m (10ft) and flowers from midsummer through to early autumn.

Growing climbers into trees need not simply mean letting them run up into the canopy. A very dramatic effect can be created by growing a bold-leaved ivy, for example *Hedera colchica* 'Sulphur Heart'♀ (**1**) (see page 101) or *Hedera colchica* 'Dentata Variegata'♀ (**2**) (see page 153), up the trunk of a forest tree such as oak (*Quercus*) or beech (*Fagus*). Ivies grow in this situation in the wild, and will therefore cope well with the dry shade at the bottom of the tree. The column of bright colour they create makes a wonderful backdrop for perennials and shrubs.

Clematis tangutica • *Clematis texensis* • *Hedera helix* 'Oro di Bogliasco' • *Humulus lupulus* 'Aureus' • *Jasminum polyanthum* •

Large green trees can tend to look dull in summer and so are wonderful hosts for big rambling roses (see pages 94–95) , for example *Rosa filipes* 'Kiftsgate'♈ (**1**), *Rosa* 'Rambling Rector'♈ and *Rosa* 'Wedding Day' (**2**). These are all very large plants growing to anything from a minimum of 7m (22ft) for 'Rambling Rector' up to a massive 17m (56ft) for 'Kiftsgate'. They all produce large clusters of white, single or semi-double flowers in summer. *Rosa* 'Bobbie James'♈ (**3**) is another excellent large, white rambler often used in trees. It has wonderful scent and grows to 10m (33ft). If you adore pink and white apple blossom colours then grow *Rosa* 'Paul's Himalayan Musk' (**4**). This gentle giant reaches 10m (33ft) tall, and in summer produces masses of rosette-shaped, very pretty pink flowers that fade as they age. It helps create a very romantic picture in any design.

All the varieties listed above are so vigorous that they really need to be left to ramble through trees for best effect. Particularly good hosts for these roses are the plane *Platanus* 'Augustine Henry' (**5**), the horse chestnut *Aesculus × carnea* 'Briotii'♈ (**6**) and the ash *Fraxinus excelsior*.

ESTABLISHING CLIMBERS IN TREES

Many people incorrectly recommend planting at the 'drip line': the line on the ground that is below the outer margin of the tree's canopy. This is where the tree's feeding roots are concentrated, forcing your climber to compete for nutrients and water. It is better to plant as near to the trunk as possible, removing a good cube of soil and mixing it with plenty of organic matter and a controlled-release fertilizer. Use common sense, though: if the ground is completely congested with roots, you will have to plant further from the trunk.

Watering regularly in the early stages will help the climber become established, after which it should be able to fend for itself. Tying the stems on to the trunk will help the climber to find its way into the canopy. Once it gets going, it will soon throw long growths across the tree and support itself.

MORE CLIMBERS FOR GROWING THROUGH SHRUBS AND TREES *Lathyrus latifolius* • *Lathyrus odoratus* •

Tropaeolum speciosum♀ (**1**), the flame creeper, is a very slender, herbaceous climber from Chile, grown from a deep-rooting, white, fleshy rhizome. Its long-spurred, nasturtium-like flowers of vibrant scarlet are borne all summer and autumn. The key to success is to keep its roots tucked away in the shade while the flowers get full sun or partial shade, so it is a prime candidate for growing through shrubs or trees. Given a deeply cultivated, moist, humus-rich, neutral to acid soil, it will grow to 3m (10ft) each season. Choose a tree or shrub with contrasting colour to show off the gorgeous flowers. The formal green hedging yew, *Taxus baccata*, is a classic choice; for a more colourful combination choose a golden form such as *Taxus baccata* Aurea Group (shown with the tropaeolum above). If the tropaeolum likes the position it is given, it will produce spherical blue fruit in autumn.

Tropaeolum tuberosum var. *lineamaculatum* 'Ken Aslet'♀ (**2**) has cup-shaped flowers, each with a long, tail-like spur; it works well on a host with a more open habit, such as *Pyracantha* or *Ceanothus* 'Pershore Zanzibar' (**3**), so the beauty of the flower shape is not lost. It is a more subtle colour than *Tropaeolum speciosum*, having warm orange petals with orange-red sepals. The flowers are produced from midsummer to late autumn and it grows to 3m (10ft).

The vine *Vitis coignetiae* (**1**) is another vigorous grower. The rounded, crinkled, matt green leaves, often lobed when young, reach 30cm (12in) across, and they turn glorious shades of crimson and scarlet in autumn (see page 145). This vine makes an impact in even really big trees, such as Turkey oak (*Quercus cerris*) (**2**), lime (*Tilia*) or ash (*Fraxinus*), where its long, trailing growths cascade down through the canopy. It will grow best in well-drained, neutral to alkaline, humus-rich soil, where it will reach 15m (50ft). For the most stunning autumn leaf colour it needs poor soil and a restricted root run, so competition from tree roots is ideal.

Lonicera × *italica* • *Parthenocissus tricuspidata* • *Passiflora caerulea* • *Rosa* 'Albertine' • *Thunbergia alata* • *Wisteria sinensis* •

Ground cover

Instead of thinking of climbers just to add vertical interest, consider using them horizontally as well. Many climbers are excellent for ground cover, some clothing very large areas with their long, trailing stems, others forming tiny mounds that are ideal for filling space at the front of a border.

Ceanothus thyrsiflorus var. repens

Large-leaved ivies make a lush carpet under trees. The golden variegation of *Hedera colchica* 'Sulphur Heart' catches the light as it breaks through the canopy above.

of foliage; in the case of evergreens, this defoliation can be permanent.

The spring-flowering **ceanothus** (see page 111) include some of the most effective ground-coverers, with attractive glossy, dark green leaves and delicious blue flowers. The best-known variety is ***Ceanothus thyrsiflorus* var. *repens*♀**. Probably the hardiest of all ceanothus, it is evergreen, fast-growing and easy to please, and bears flowers in mid-spring from an early age. It covers an area of 2.5m (8ft) and grows to 1m (40in) high.

The primary advantage of climbers used as ground cover is their low profile. They hug the contours of the land and can cover ground underneath shrubs better than traditional ground-cover plants. They are suitable for use in all styles of planting, from woodland gardens to traditional mixed borders.

Some climbers root as they grow and provide very thick, impenetrable cover. They also clothe inaccessible sites, such as banks and scrubby areas, very effectively. When planting them, pin the stems out in a cartwheel shape to encourage the shoots to root at the nodes and spread out as quickly as possible.

Other climbers will benefit from being planted through a layer of weed-control matting. Weeds can be very damaging, smothering ornamental plants and competing with them for air and water as well as light, which may result in loss

---

YEAR-ROUND GROUND COVER

By planting two climbers together as ground cover – for example, small-leaved ivies and delicate clematis species, like *Clematis viticella* – you can have weed-suppressing colour all year round. Combine these with a careful choice of spring bulbs and the space will really work hard for you.

MORE CLIMBERS FOR GROUND COVER *Clematis montana* • *Cotoneaster horizontalis* • *Eccremocarpus scaber* •

Ceanothus 'Centennial' is a more slender, delicate grower with tiny, very dark green leaves and small, darkest blue flowers in late spring. It is low-growing, at 30cm (12in), and reaches 4m (13ft) across, and the evergreen foliage makes an ideal foil for another flowering climber. It loves the sun and needs a fertile, well-drained soil. (See Good Companions, below.)

Clematis viticella hybrids (see also page 139) are vigorous and easy to grow. Although not leafy enough to completely cover the ground on their own, they can be threaded through other shrubs to give added interest. Prostrate conifers like *Juniperus procumbens* and *Juniperus squamata* 'Blue Carpet'♔ and coloured foliage heathers make ideal hosts.

Clematis 'Alba Luxurians'♔ has nodding, papery white flowers, borne profusely through midsummer to early autumn. It grows to 3m (10ft) and needs to be planted where the stems can be led onto the host plant so that when in flower they are at the focal point of the planting scheme.

Clematis 'Madame Julia Correvon'♔, another viticella hybrid of the same size, produces particularly charming rich red flowers with slightly twisted sepals and splayed stamens.

The hardy forms of ivy (*Hedera*), including the variegated varieties of the large-leaved *Hedera colchica* (see pages 152–53), provide effective evergreen ground cover, and all will stand full shade, poor soil and dry conditions. The English ivy, *Hedera helix*, gives a fantastic cover of rich green foliage. Where the vigour of the species would be too great there are many cultivars with a much slower rate of growth, suitable for even the smallest of spaces. *Hedera helix* 'Spetchley'♔ is a dense, prostrate plant, reaching just 15cm (6in), with very small, green leaves, and is ideal for ground cover in the border. *Hedera helix* 'Ivalace'♔ is larger, spreading to 1m (40in), with glossy, rich green leaves with a curled edge. Mound-forming *Hedera helix* 'Little Diamond', growing to just 30cm (12in), has diamond-shaped, grey-green leaves with creamy-white margins; it is small enough to take a place in the front of a border with heucheras or ajugas.

Like the English ivy, *Lonicera japonica* (Japanese honeysuckle) is a vigorous plant and it roots as it grows, meaning it can quickly cover very wide areas. Its young shoots are tinged with purple and it has very richly fragrant, creamy-white flowers often flushed purple on the outside. It grows to 6m (20ft) and makes excellent ground cover for inaccessible banks. The cultivar *Lonicera japonica* 'Dart's World' has a spreading, bushy habit. The flowers are unusual in being white flushed with red when they first open but later fading to cream.

Hard landscaping looks wonderful with its edges softened by elegant trails of ivy. A simple planting of *Hedera helix* (English ivy) makes these steps even more attractive.

Clematis 'Madame Julia Correvon'

Hedera helix 'Ivalace'

GOOD COMPANIONS

The rich plum-coloured foliage of *Berberis thunbergii* f. *atropurpurea* (1) looks fabulous underplanted with a deep blue carpet of *Ceanothus* 'Centennial' (2).

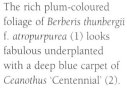

Euonymus fortunei • Muehlenbeckia complexa • Humulus lupulus 'Aureus' • Tropaeolum majus •

Screens and dividers

The majority of gardens have something that needs screening from view – an oil tank, a compost bin or dustbin area, or a neighbouring house. Quick screens are particularly necessary in new gardens to provide privacy and much appreciated colour until permanent plantings become established. Long-term screens can also be used to divide a garden into smaller areas, or simply to serve as a living backdrop for other plants.

The bold, dramatic flowers of the fast-growing *Eccremocarpus scaber* scramble through the rich purple and cream flowers of *Clematis florida* var. *sieboldiana*, creating a quick temporary screen.

QUICK, TEMPORARY SCREENS

Annual climbers grow fast and flower within the year, making them ideal subjects for providing a quick, temporary screen. They are usually easy to raise from seed, but not everyone has either the facilities or, more frankly, the inclination to do this. A packet of seeds may seem good value, but do you really need 20 or more plants of the same climber? There is also the cost of a bag of compost and pots to take into account. Alternatively you can sow direct into the ground, although this will result in later flowers.

Buying annual climbers in pots from a garden centre or nursery means that all the initial work has been done: raised in optimum conditions, plants should be

Cobaea scandens

MORE DECIDUOUS CLIMBERS FOR SCREENS *Akebia quinata* • *Clematis alpina* • *Clematis macropetala* •

healthy, bushy and raring to go. Garden centres today offer a wide range of annual climbers including an increasing number of older, more interesting varieties.

Commonly known as cathedral bells or cup and saucer plant, *Cobaea scandens*♀ is one of the best annuals for screening. In its home land of Mexico, where it is perennial, this tendril climber can reach up to 20m (65ft). As an annual in colder climates it grows to 3m (10ft). It loves full sun and good humidity and prefers an alkaline soil. Because it is so vigorous it benefits from plenty of food: a liquid feed twice a week will bring out the best in it. The bell-shaped flowers are initially greenish white, ageing to a rich, dusky rose-purple, and are produced among the green, pinnate leaves from midsummer right until the frosts; they are followed in early autumn by egg-shaped fruit.

Eccremocarpus scaber (Chilean glory flower) can be difficult to find in nurseries but it is certainly worth the effort. It likes fertile, well-drained soil with plenty of sun. If it enjoys the conditions provided, it will be a herbaceous perennial (albeit short-lived); otherwise it will be an annual. A tendril climber reaching 4.5m (15ft) high, it has small, bright green, pinnate leaves. The long, tubular flowers, pollinated in the wild by hummingbirds, are orange-red with an orange, turned-back tip. Other colours are also available, including rich vibrant orange, bright pink to pink-red,

Ipomoea tricolor 'Heavenly Blue'

scarlet tipped with orange, rich golden yellow, and a stunning cream.

The morning glory *Ipomoea tricolor* **'Heavenly Blue'** seldom fails to attract attention. The funnel-shaped flowers are a sensational shade of azure with a white throat. In the tropics and in a conservatory, this fast-growing twiner is a short-lived perennial and will flower throughout the year; in colder climates, it is an annual and flowers all summer. Given a sheltered position in fertile soil with full sun, it will grow to 3–4m (10–13ft) before frost catches up with it.

Lathyrus odoratus 'Matucana'

Lathyrus odoratus (sweet pea), another tendril climber, is considered a classic of the English summer garden although it comes originally from Italy and Sicily. Modern varieties tend to have large, fancy flowers in icing-sugar colours and with relatively little fragrance; older hybrids, often sold as 'antique' sweet peas, have smaller, richly scented, more vibrant flowers. These sit more happily in an informal garden setting, and are once again becoming more widely available. *Lathyrus odoratus* **'Lord Nelson'** is a rich, clear blue; *Lathyrus odoratus* **'Matucana'** has two-tone flowers in maroon-purple and deep purple-blue. Sweet peas need moist but well-drained, fertile soil, in a sunny site. Regular watering is important to prevent powdery mildew. (See Good Companions, page 76.)

(See Good Companions, page 76.)

USING ANNUAL CLIMBERS

There are two ways of using annual climbers for screening and the choice will depend on how advanced your planting is. If your garden is brand new and features such as trellis screen are not yet in place, then use stout rustic poles at 2m (6ft) intervals and staple cheap plastic bean netting to the posts. At the end of the season when your annuals begin to die back you can simply cut the netting down and dispose of it and the plant material together.

If trellis screens are already in position and the permanent planting is in but has yet to get properly under way, then run annual climbers up the trellis. It takes a little more time to clear away the spent growth at the end of the season, but the results will look so good that you may be tempted to keep growing annuals in this way even when your perennial climbers are established.

Hydrangea anomala subsp. *petiolaris* • *Muehlenbeckia complexa* • *Parthenocissus tricuspidata* 'Veitchii' • *Wisteria sinensis* •

Clematis cirrhosa

Hedera hibernica

Passiflora caerulea

PERMANENT SCREENS

Many evergreen climbers are excellent plants for creating permanent screens. They take up a great deal less space than traditional evergreen hedging plants and so are much more in keeping with today's smaller gardens.

Clematis cirrhosa (see page 150) has good, close-knit, evergreen foliage with the added advantage of gently nodding, creamy, bell-shaped flowers through the winter. It grows to 4m (13ft) and is ideal for covering trellis panels.

Hedera hibernica♀, the Irish ivy, is widely used commercially because it is fast-growing and easy to look after. The rich, dark foliage makes a good background for more vibrant colours. If your screen is intended to divide the garden rather than act as a backdrop, consider using variegated ivies, such as *Hedera helix* 'Goldchild'♀ or *Hedera colchica* 'Dentata Variegata'♀ (see pages 101 and 153). They are very effective and provide welcome winter colour.

For a sunny position the blue passion flower *Passiflora caerulea*♀ gives a very exotic look, with its bold, white and blue flowers borne from summer through to autumn, and ornamental orange fruit that mingle with the late blooms. It will reach 10m (33ft) and provide relatively thin cover, which allows plenty of light through, making it the ideal plant for screening a swimming pool or seating area. (See Good Companions, below, and see page 141.)

SUPPORTS FOR PERMANENT SCREENS

Permanent screens are best created using a heavyweight trellis supported between wooden uprights. To give an illusion of depth, run a top rail between the two supports and put 45cm (18in) cross beams along the top. This is called a single pergola and gives the impression of a full-width pergola, making small gardens appear bigger.

Fruit trained to form a screen is best supported on a tall post and wire fence; this allows air to circulate and the sun to fall on the fruit.

GOOD COMPANIONS

In mid- to late summer *Clematis* 'Victoria'♀ (1) adds extra colour to a screen of the white-flowering, richly scented, evergreen *Trachelospermum asiaticum*♀ (2).

Runner beans (*Phaseolus coccineus*) trained on rows of bamboo canes make an excellent summer screen. For extra scent run *Lathyrus odoratus* 'Cupani' through the rows. (3)

Lavandula 'Tiara' (4) will make a neat edging at the base of a screen of *Passiflora caerulea*♀ (5) and will revel in the same hot, dry, sunny conditions.

MORE EVERGREEN CLIMBERS FOR SCREENS *Euonymus fortunei* 'Emerald 'n' Gold' • *Lonicera henryi* •

For summer-long, white, starry flowers above evergreen foliage both *Solanum laxum* 'Album'♀ and *Trachelospermum asiaticum*♀ are recommended. Both are slender growers and make ideal screens. (See Good Companions, left, and see pages 41 and 81.)

Less formal screens can be created using deciduous plants. The advantages of these are twofold. They have a softer appearance, well suited to country gardens. Also, if low light levels in winter are a problem, deciduous climbers will provide a screen in summer, while letting in much more light in winter, after the leaves have dropped and when the need for privacy is not so great. *Clematis montana* (see pages 48 and 123) is very effective, as is *Fallopia baldschuanica*, the Russian vine or mile a minute (see page 52). For a very contemporary look *Muehlenbeckia complexa* is well worth seeking out. A twining climber, it has wiry stems with minute, rounded, green leaves. The tangled mass of growth, 3m (10ft) tall, makes a wonderful screen, while the tiny, cup-shaped, greenish-white flowers add their sweet scent to the picture in summer.

As well as being excellent wall plants, trained **fruit trees** make lovely informal screens, their rustic charm adding character to a garden. The tree is trained on a post and wire framework into one of a number of different shapes, depending

Solanum laxum 'Album'

Clematis montana var. rubens 'Tetrarose'

Fallopia baldschuanica

on the space available. In a small garden a cordon is most suitable, where the tree is trained on a single stem at a 45° angle. Larger gardens can accommodate a fan shape, with branches radiating from a low central point, or an espalier, either a central stem with three branches on each

side at an angle of 90° or a low horizontal branch each side of the main stem with vertical branches rising from this at 90°. Whichever form you choose, the tree will need spur pruning, similar to that for a wisteria, to maintain the shape and promote fruiting (see pages 34, 35).

FRUIT FOR SCREENS

Apples, pears, plums, cherries, figs and virtually any other tree fruit are suitable for training to make screens. Apricots, peaches and nectarines can also be grown in this way, but these need lavish attention and in cooler climates rarely give a decent crop in return.

Many fruit trees must be pollinated by a different variety, so you will need at least two trees that flower at the same time. Those that need no pollinator are called self-fertile and are the best choice for small gardens.

Pyracantha 'Orange Glow' • *Solanum laxum* 'Album Variegatum' • *Trachelospermum jasminoides* 'Wilsonii' •

Pots and containers

Pots are indispensable: they add so much to any garden design. They help to create an atmosphere, and are also wonderfully flexible, enabling you to move plants in and out of a planting scheme. Containers allow you to grow climbers that don't suit the soil in your garden and – perhaps most importantly – they even enable you to grow climbers where there is no soil at all.

The free-flowering *Clematis* 'H.F. Young' and the big double-flowered *Clematis* 'Duchess of Edinburgh' spiral around an obelisk in a pot, creating a soft, romantic look.

ivy need the support of obelisks, arches and fan trellis. Give as much thought to the support as to the pot. The style must match, and the structure needs to be durable for slow-growing subjects; fast growers or annuals can be grown through short-lived, woven willow frameworks.

PERENNIAL CLIMBERS FOR POTS

Flowers are especially important for adding atmosphere. The bold Mediterranean-style colour of **bougainvilleas** (see page 59) will give an exotic feel to a sun-drenched area. They will need the protection of a conservatory in winter, but the long flowering period in summer and autumn makes up for this inconvenience. When confined to a pot, bougainvillea grows to 4m (13ft) or so. It can be tucked out of the way when it pauses in its flowering in midsummer and brought back to join

Choosing the right plant for the right pot is the key to success. Design is the first consideration: the usual advice is to use containers that are in keeping with the style of the garden. Size is the next: plants will always do better in larger pots. When deciding where to put pots, remember that just one container thoughtfully planted and positioned can serve as a focal point. If you want several pots, bear in mind that a few large, matching or toning containers grouped in one part of the garden will be more effective than lots of small ones all of different designs scattered over a large area.

Groups of pots need some structure to be successful. Stiffly branched climbers and wall shrubs, such as pyracantha, ceanothus and chaenomeles, can be trained into formal shapes such as cones, fans or espaliers. Soft-stemmed climbers, such as trachelospermum, clematis and

DESIGNING WITH POTS

• Pots in groups look best if they are all similar in design and construction.

• Traditional settings demand classic, quality pots, while contemporary minimalist gardens can accommodate sculptural containers with simple lines and using innovative materials.

• Rustic gardens require everyday containers sympathetic to their environment.

• Suburban gardens need timeless pots, perhaps with a sense of fun.

PLANTING CLEMATIS AND IVY IN A POT WITH AN OBELISK

Place pot feet beneath the pot to keep it level and assist drainage.

Place crocks on the pot base and part-fill the pot with soil-based compost.

Very carefully slide the ivy out of its pot, keeping the rootball intact.

Place the ivy on the firmed soil in the new pot. Ensure the plant is straight.

Gently remove the clematis from its pot. Again, keep the rootball intact.

Plant the clematis in the new pot, positioning it carefully.

Untie the stems from the cane and remove the cane.

Fill around the plants with more compost to just below the pot's rim.

Carefully lay the plants flat and insert the obelisk into the compost.

Wind the ivy round the obelisk so the stems will grow upwards in a spiral.

Carefully train the clematis round the obelisk verticals in a spiral pattern.

Finally, give the plants a really thorough soaking with water.

TIPS FOR CHOOSING AND USING POTS

• A pot with a flared top allows the plant to be repotted more easily.

• A larger pot helps protect the plant's roots from high and low temperatures.

• A clay pot 'breathes', allowing more air to the plant's roots.

• Soil-based compost is best for long-term planting.

• Plenty of crocks in the base maintain good drainage.

• A mulch on the top of the compost helps it retain water.

• Raising the pot off the ground aids drainage and prevents waterlogging.

CARING FOR PLANTS IN POTS

A good soil-based compost is the starting point for pots – it holds more nutrients than a soil-less compost. A plant can stay in the same pot for many years but will need annual feeding with a slow- or controlled-release fertilizer. Scraping off and replacing the top few centimetres of compost also helps to keep older plants growing happily.

Regular and sufficient watering is essential. For a number of pots, consider automatic irrigation: it may seem excessive, but in the height of summer it will mean that you are sitting enjoying your pots rather than endlessly watering them. It is also far more water-efficient, as it directs a much smaller jet of water directly onto the compost, ensuring it is absorbed properly rather than running over the edges of the pot. A thick layer of mulch material, such as hardwood chips, slate, crushed glass or simple garden compost, will help conserve the water that you do add.

the rest of the display when it begins to bloom again. There are many different varieties, usually sold as houseplants; those with deep purple-pink flowers are the easiest, while the more unusual apricots and creams are best left to more experienced growers.

Camellias (see page 117) are valuable for their glossy, deep green, evergreen foliage and glamorous spring flowers.

Camellia × williamsii 'E.G. Waterhouse'

Camellia × williamsii 'Golden Spangles'

Camellia × williamsii 'Saint Ewe'

CLEMATIS FOR POTS

Some clematis work exceptionally well in pots, especially on obelisks, which will give their soft growth plenty of support. Clematis that build up a framework of branches, such as the early and mid-season hybrids, are the easiest to train.

If you want a really good show, plant two of the same variety in one pot. Train the stems round and round an obelisk, working in a spiral pattern to spread the flower buds evenly. Pruning is quite simple: wait until late winter then trim back to fat, green buds; tie in new growth as it appears.

Clematis ANNA LOUISE (**'Evithree'**)♛ (**1**) Large, velvety purple flowers with a broad red stripe. Flowers from late spring right through to early autumn. Height 2.5m (8ft).

Clematis **'Asao'** (**2**) Attractive young foliage flushed with bronze. Flowers are deep pink, paling towards the centre of each sepal, with yellow anthers. Height 2.5m (8ft).

Clematis **'Edith'**♛ (**3**) Large, white flowers with a green flush and deep red anthers; similar in shape to the pale lavender *Clematis* **'Mrs Cholmondeley'**♛ (see page 121). Height 2m (6ft).

Clematis EVENING STAR (**'Evista'**) Pointed, twisted sepals of a strong purple-mauve with a deep cerise bar and golden anthers. Height 3m (10ft).

Clematis **'The President'**♛ (**4**) Vibrant, deep purple-blue flowers, silvery on the reverse, from late spring right through to early autumn. Height 3m (10ft).

camellias are allowed to dry out or suffer erratic watering in late summer, they will drop their flower buds. The *Camellia × williamsii* hybrids are probably the most effective in pots as they flower very freely and, unlike *Camellia japonica* hybrids, they drop the blooms as they fade, allowing new buds to take their place. Excellent subjects for pots include: *Camellia × williamsii* **'Anticipation'**♛, with dark pink, peony-form flowers; *Camellia × williamsii* **'Donation'**♛, a semi-double, pale pink; *Camellia × williamsii* **'E.G. Waterhouse'**, with shell-pink, formal double flowers; *Camellia × williamsii* **'Golden Spangles'**, a single, bright pink with gold-splashed leaves; and *Camellia × williamsii* **'Saint Ewe'**♛, an early single pink.

Passion flowers (*Passiflora*) have large, showy blooms that bring a feeling of the tropics to a sunny sheltered corner (see page 141). *Passiflora* **'Eden'** bears soft lavender flowers, edged with amethyst, from midsummer through to the frosts. It must have a poor, well-drained, neutral soil to do well. A vigorous climber, it will reach 6m (20ft) but needs support.

Their very fine root system suits pot culture and even gardeners on chalk soil can grow these lime-hating shrubs extremely successfully in pots using an ericaceous loam-based compost.

Container growing tends to create more compact plants of 2–3m (6–10ft). Watering is key to good flowering; if

ANNUAL CLIMBERS

Annual climbers that give a blaze of colour have an exuberance that can really add charm to a group of pots. The sweet pea, *Lathyrus odoratus*, is the classic choice (see pages 75 and 133). In the confines of a patio the big, showy blooms of the modern hybrids really come into their own. The sheer size and quantity of flowers they produce make them equal partners with summer bedding plants.

Thunbergia alata (black-eyed Susan) is a perennial in its native tropical Africa; in cooler, temperate climates, it is very successful as an annual, twining its stems round its support to reach 2.5m (8ft) in height. The large, yellow or orange flowers have a chocolate-purple eye and are freely produced from summer through to autumn. Give it a site where it will be shaded from the hottest sun. Take cuttings towards the end of the season to ensure young plants for the next year, or raise new plants from seed.

Thunbergia alata

Tropaeolum peregrinum, the canary creeper, is rather exotic in appearance. The bright yellow flowers have large, fringed upper petals that look just like a bird's wings. It comes from Ecuador and Peru and thrives in full sun. It flowers all summer and autumn and, depending on the season, it can reach 2.5–4m (8–13ft) tall. Another tropaeolum with a completely different style is **Tropaeolum majus**, better known as the nasturtium. We have, perhaps, grown rather too familiar with the stunted dwarf varieties, but the nasturtium is by nature a climber. Look out for the varieties *Tropaeolum majus* 'Jewel of Africa' and *Tropaeolum majus* 'Tall Single Mixed'; they will produce masses of orange, red or yellow flowers all summer and autumn.

EDIBLE PLANTS

Always have a pot of nasturtiums (*Tropaeolum majus*) near the kitchen and you can add the peppery leaves and flowers to salads. You can even eat the young fruit. Plant the annual *Borago officinalis* at the base and you can use the stunning blue borage flowers too; they look pretty frozen in ice cubes in summer drinks.

THE IMPORTANCE OF FOLIAGE

Foliage contributes a good deal to the success of pots. Within a group, try to ensure that you have variation in leaf size and shape. Large-leaved climbers, such as *Hedera colchica* 'Dentata'♀ (see page 153), give important contrast to small foliage, for example that of *Billardiera longiflora*♀ (see page 55). Plants with variegated foliage, such as *Solanum laxum* 'Album Variegatum' (**1**), can also lighten the overall effect of a group of pots, giving the impression of depth.

Filling all your pots with gorgeous flowering climbers is a common pitfall. They will look wonderful for a few weeks of the year, but then you have a long wait for them to perform again. Spare a couple of pots for evergreens, for example *Clematis cirrhosa*, *Trachelospermum asiaticum*♀ (**2**) and ivy (*Hedera*). They give structure and interest even when not in flower or berry. They also act as a permanent, solid background for flowering climbers. (See also page 76.)

Clay soil

Heavy, difficult to work, waterlogged in winter, baked hard in summer – these are the most familiar descriptions of clay. But the truth is that clay is a very fertile soil, holding nutrients well, and, once established, climbers do very well in it.

Lonicera sempervirens

Bold, dramatic *Actinidia kolomikta* is one of many climbers that thrive on clay once they are established.

The trouble with clay soil is that it has very tiny particles that stick together, impeding the flow of air and water. Adding lime will encourage the clay particles to cling together in larger groups, giving a more crumbly, open texture, but it does affect the soil pH. The most effective way of improving clay soil is by adding bulky organic matter, such as well-rotted garden compost or manure. (See page 23.)

Double digging initially will break up the subsoil, improving the drainage. It will also allow you to add plenty of organic matter to the topsoil. Incorporating compost or manure into the soil when planting, and using it generously as a mulch afterwards, will also pay dividends. By doing this, you can widen your choice of climbers from just a handful to all but Mediterranean-type climbers that need dry soil in winter.

The **honeysuckles** (*Lonicera*) are among the most beautiful of climbers and they all thrive in clay. The biggest mistake when growing honeysuckles is to give them a hot, sunny position. They are woodland plants and like dappled shade and a cool root run. The following are just two of the species commonly cultivated. For a more extensive range of honeysuckles, see pages 128–29.

Lonicera periclymenum (common honeysuckle) is a sweetly scented, deciduous, twining climber, reaching 7m (22ft), with creamy-yellow flowers flushed with pink in mid- and late summer. *Lonicera periclymenum* 'Red Gables' (see Good Companions, page 85) has cream-coloured flowers flushed with deep red. It is very similar to *Lonicera periclymenum* 'Serotina'♛ (see page 129), but is neater and more compact, reaching just 5m (16ft).

Lonicera sempervirens♛, the trumpet honeysuckle, is semi-evergreen and has dramatic, orange-scarlet flowers with golden yellow insides. It is very hardy, and is resistant to aphids, unlike its hybrid *Lonicera × brownii* 'Dropmore Scarlet' (see page 107). It grows to a height of 4m (13ft) and flowers from early summer through to late autumn.

OTHER GOOD CLIMBERS FOR CLAY *Celastrus orbiculatus* • *Clematis alpina* • *Clematis macropetala* •

FOLIAGE CLIMBERS FOR CLAY

Actinidia kolomikta♀ (see left and see also page 116). A deciduous twiner with bold green leaves tipped pink and white. Insignificant white or pink flowers in early summer. Height 4.5m (15ft).

Akebia quinata (1) (see also pages 50 and 104). Most commonly grown for its deep purple, cocoa-scented flowers but it also has attractive, architectural, five-lobed,

matt green foliage. A semi-evergreen twiner reaching 10m (33ft).

Ampelopsis brevipedunculata (2) (see also pages 142–43). A handsome, deciduous, vine-like climber growing to 5m (16ft). Rich autumn colours and blue fruit.

Parthenocissus henryana♀ (3) (see also page 147). Dainty, silver-veined, green

leaves, sometimes with a pink flush. Excellent red autumn colour. A self-clinging climber, growing to 10m (33ft).

Schizophragma hydrangeoides 'Moonlight' (4) (see also page 45). Bold, deciduous, silvery leaves with green veins. Creamy, lacecap flowers in midsummer. Good yellow autumn colour. Aerial rooting, growing to 12m (40ft).

FLOWERING CLIMBERS AND WALL SHRUBS FOR CLAY

Campsis × *tagliabuana* 'Madame Galen'♀ (1) (see also page 39). Rich, warm orange, tubular blooms produced from late summer to autumn. Deciduous pinnate foliage. Aerial rooting. Grows to 10m (33ft).

Chaenomeles speciosa 'Yukigoten' (2) (see also page 118). A wall shrub that

bears semi-double, alabaster flowers in spring followed by aromatic yellow fruit. Height 4m (13ft).

Fallopia baldschuanica (3) (see also page 52). Vigorous, deciduous, twining climber (known as mile a minute), growing to 15m (50ft). In late summer and autumn it is buried under a sea of foamy white flowers.

Solanum crispum 'Glasnevin'♀ (see page 41). A semi-evergreen, shrubby, scrambling climber with mauve, potato-like flowers all summer. Grows to 6m (20ft).

Wisteria 'Burford' (4) (see also page 125). Heavily scented, rich purple and lilac flowers in late spring and early summer. Good autumn colour. Grows to 9m (30ft).

Hedera colchica 'Dentata' • *Hedera helix* • *Humulus lupulus* 'Aureus' • *Hydrangea anomala* subsp. *petiolaris* •

Rosa 'Blairii Number Two'

Rosa 'Climbing Crimson Glory'

Rosa 'Climbing Paul Lédé'

Rosa 'Compassion'

Rosa 'Golden Showers'

Rosa 'Sombreuil'

All **roses** thrive in clay soil. They love the abundance of nutrients, which feeds their long flowering season. Both climbing roses and ramblers will be happy in clay with a little organic matter added at planting time, as will English roses grown as climbers. The following is but a tiny sample of the many varieties available; for other climbing and rambling roses, see pages 130–32.

Climbing roses build up a framework of flowering shoots and grow to an average height of 3–5m (10–16ft). Flowering is primarily in early summer, with some varieties producing flowers on and off throughout the season. Some climbing roses are old Victorian cultivars; others are more recent.

Dating from the 1860s, *Rosa* 'Blairii Number Two'♥ has glorious, richly scented, deeply cupped, old-fashioned flowers, deep pink in the centre, fading at the edges, so perfect that they look as if they were made from sugar. It needs very little fuss, reaches 5m (16ft) and looks lovely growing casually through open fencing. It blooms mainly in early summer with a few flowers later in the season. (See Good Companions, right.)

A much younger rose is *Rosa* 'Compassion'♥, introduced in the early 1970s. In summer it has sweetly scented, hybrid tea flowers of salmon-pink with a flush of apricot in the centre. Unlike many newer climbers, it has plenty of good glossy foliage and strong, bushy growth up to 3.5m (12ft) high. It is an excellent rose, one of the best.

Red roses can sometimes be disappointing: lacking in scent, often more tender than their pink counterparts and with a weaker constitution. *Rosa* 'Climbing Crimson Glory' is an exception. It has large, deep crimson, hybrid tea flowers with a gorgeous, strong old rose fragrance. It grows to 5m (16ft), is a good climber for a pillar and makes a superb host for a clematis. It flowers in early summer with a few later blooms.

Rosa 'Golden Showers'♥ is one of the best roses for a shady wall (see page 45). Growing to a neat 3.5m (12ft), and lightly fragrant, it flowers very freely all summer, producing large, semi-double, golden blooms, with spidery stamens that fade to creamy primrose with age. It will need to be planted in good soil to perform well.

The tea rose fragrance encapsulates the classic English rose scent and *Rosa* 'Climbing Paul Lédé' has it in abundance. The flowers are rich biscuity apricot, deeper in the centre and flushed with pink, and are produced continuously all summer. It grows to 4m (13ft) and is vigorous and extremely hardy.

OTHER GOOD CLIMBERS AND WALL SHRUBS FOR CLAY *Jasminum officinale* • *Parthenocissus quinquefolia* •

Rosa 'Sombreuil' is another really hardy tea rose, with flat, quartered, rosette-shaped flowers of milky white with a faint hint of pink. It is a neat grower, reaching just 4m (13ft), and ideal for a pillar or arch. Its richly scented blooms are produced throughout the summer and it has remained popular since its introduction in 1850. (See Good Companions, below.)

Rambling roses produce new shoots from ground level every year and grow to an average height of 5–10m (16–33ft). Most have only one flush of flower, in early and midsummer. Choose with care as most need plenty of space.

Rosa 'Crimson Shower'♥ is an elegant rambler with dark, glossy foliage and lightly scented, rich crimson, double flowers. The golden stamens in the centre ensure that the flowers do not become too heavy in colour, and the occasional flash of white from the base of the petals adds to this overall feeling of lightness.

Rosa 'Crimson Shower'

Growing to 5m (16ft), this rose starts flowering in midsummer and continues into early autumn.

Rosa 'Goldfinch' is an unsung hero in the rose world. It is tough and disease resistant and survives in even the most difficult situation. It is not particularly tall, reaching just 3.5m (12ft), and in early and midsummer has large clusters of egg-yellow flowers that fade to creamy white, with a strong tea rose scent.

Rosa 'Phyllis Bide'

Rosa 'Phyllis Bide'♥ is an unusual rambler: its growth is flower-packed and it repeats freely throughout the season. Its compact size, just 3.5m (12ft), and the abundance of flower make it an ideal choice for a pillar or pergola post. The small, scented, loosely formed flowers are yellow with a pinkish-apricot centre. As the flower fades the centre lightens to lemon-yellow and the outer petals take on pink markings.

GOOD COMPANIONS

Alchemilla mollis♥ (lady's mantle) (1) is excellent planted at the foot of many roses, for example *Rosa* 'Sombreuil' (2), creating a soft, romantic feel.

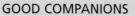

Salvia officinalis 'Purpurascens'♥ (3) makes an aromatic companion for *Rosa* 'Blairii Number Two'♥ (4) and thrives in the same sunny position.

Lonicera periclymenum 'Red Gables' (5) is a perfect host for *Clematis* 'Polish Spirit'♥ (6), an easy to grow hybrid that comes into flower as the honeysuckle fades.

BLACK SPOT

Black spot is a fungal disease of roses spread by spores on the leaves. In rainy weather the spores are spread by water splash. If left unchecked it can completely defoliate roses, weakening them fatally in the long term. The disease shows up as black round spots on the leaves, which then turn yellow and drop. It can spread to the stems.

Treatment involves spraying with a fungicide; this will not cure the existing problem but will prevent further infection. It is best to remove and burn all affected foliage.

Removing any fallen leaves around the base of plants in autumn is a wise precaution since these will harbour spores. Cutting out affected stems will also help. A preventative spray with fungicide is very effective but must be applied at fortnightly intervals, starting as the plant comes into leaf.

Pileostegia viburnoides • *Pyracantha* 'Soleil d'Or' • *Sophora* SUN KING ('Hilsop') • *Trachelospermum jasminoides* • *Vitis* 'Brant' •

Chalky soil

Chalky soil may be a challenge, but it is never a hopeless case. On the positive side, soils over chalk drain well and are relatively warm, making them ideal for Mediterranean-type plants. On the negative side, the lime in the soil breaks down nutrients very quickly and these tend to be rapidly washed away. Adding bulky organic material will help to improve chalky soils, making them much more hospitable to a wide range of plants.

A shimmer of hazy blue flowers makes *Ceanothus* 'Delight' a classic choice of elegant wall shrub for a chalky soil.

Adding bulky organic matter in the form of well-rotted manure or garden compost will do much to improve chalky soils, helping them to retain both moisture and nutrients. The drawback is that the lime in the soil speeds up the action of bacteria, encouraging this same organic matter to decompose. The only solution to this is adding compost or manure every year, either digging it in or using it as a mulch.

If you do this, all but the very thinnest of soils over chalk will support the California lilacs, **ceanothus** (see page 111). Their flowers appear in every shade of blue, from palest powder blue to rich, intense deep blue. There are also white and pink cultivars, although their appeal is rather limited. Ceanothus grow rapidly, reaching an average height of 4m (13ft) with the help of a warm wall, and are

excellent shrubs for new houses whe quick colour is a priority.

Ceanothus hybrids have very mixe parentage, and their hardiness vari considerably. One of the hardiest *Ceanothus* 'Delight', which has panicl of rich blue flowers in late spring th contrast well with the glossy, evergree foliage. The habit is elegant, with gen arching branches.

Ceanothus impressus

Ceanothus thyrsiflorus 'Skylark'

blue flowers are produced in mid- to late spring from rusty-coloured buds.

Ceanothus thyrsiflorus 'Skylark'♀ has a neat, upright habit with masses of deep blue flowers in late spring and early summer, set against glossy, evergreen foliage. (See Good Companions, below.)

Most **cotoneasters** love chalky soils, thriving in the poor conditions.

Probably the toughest of all ceanothus is the evergreen **Ceanothus impressus**, the Santa Barbara ceanothus. It has very small green leaves and a twiggy, stiff habit of growth; slightly more compact than other varieties, it reaches 3m (10ft). The clear

CLEMATIS AND CHALK

One of the most commonly held incorrect beliefs about clematis is that they must be grown in chalky soil. This probably stems from the fact that the native *Clematis vitalba* (old man's beard or traveller's joy) was used historically as a rootstock for large-flowered hybrids and itself occurs naturally on thin, chalky soils.

There is no evidence, however, that clematis need chalk. In fact they grow perfectly happily on neutral and acid soils. More important is a good rich soil, with plenty of moisture available yet being well drained. Sandy soils drain too quickly for clematis and heavy clay soils are too wet and cold in winter for fine-rooted varieties.

GOOD COMPANIONS

Thread *Clematis* 'Huldine'♀ (1), with its delicate, pearly-white flowers, through *Ceanothus thyrsiflorus* 'Skylark'♀ (2) to extend the period of interest right through to the end of summer.

Let *Trachelospermum asiaticum*♀ (3) blend with *Euonymus fortunei* 'Emerald Gaiety'♀ (4) to give year-round interest, with deliciously scented flowers in summer and coloured foliage all winter.

Forsythia suspensa (5) will create a cloud of clear yellow flowers above the blue spikes of the aromatic shrub *Rosmarinus officinalis* (6) in early spring.

Cotoneaster horizontalis

Cotoneaster atropurpureus 'Variegatus'

Cotoneaster horizontalis♀ is a classic wall shrub, especially good for low walls. It will also cope well with shade. It has tiny, wavy-edged, green leaves on stiffly arching branches arranged in a distinctive herringbone pattern. Dainty white flowers open from sugar-pink buds nestling along the branches in early summer. In autumn the leaves colour well before falling and the older branches are covered with lines of rich red berries.

If you want to use a variegated plant consider **Cotoneaster atropurpureus 'Variegatus'**♀. It was long thought to be a variety of *Cotoneaster horizontalis*, but does not have the same herringbone arrangement of leaves and has been renamed. The deciduous leaves are green, edged with cream and flushed with rich red in autumn. Simple white flowers are produced all over the plant in early summer. Both these cotoneasters grow naturally to 2m (6ft), but if trained up a framework can reach 3m (10ft).

For self-clinging colour, the climbing forms of the shrubby evergreen **Euonymus fortunei** are extremely successful and are a welcome change from ivy. The Japanese variety of the species, *Euonymus fortunei* var. *radicans*, is the source of these. They are hardier than ivy, making them extremely popular in North America.

Climbing by aerial roots, they initially need tying to their support to encourage the roots to cling firmly to the surface. Like ivy, they climb with their juvenile growth and bear flowers only on their adult growth. The flowers, not as showy as those of ivy, are pale green, and sometimes produce pinkish capsules with orange seeds.

One of the most useful shrubs in the garden, **Euonymus fortunei 'Emerald Gaiety'**♀ has grey-green leaves edged with milky white. On chalky or sandy, well-drained soil the foliage tends to have a pink flush. (See Good Companions, page 87.) **Euonymus fortunei 'Emerald 'n' Gold'**♀ is another excellent shrub that happily climbs when given the chance, but this cultivar has bright green leaves edged with rich golden yellow (see page 48). In winter the leaves often take on a flush of red. Both these are evergreen and reach a height of 3m (10ft).

Euonymus fortunei 'Silver Queen' is a larger-leaved variety, also reaching 3m (10ft). This is a superb garden plant and makes a wonderful small climber. It has evergreen, grey-green leaves edged with creamy white and looks stunning growing casually across a small wall or fence.

For spring effect **Forsythia suspensa** is delightful. A large, deciduous shrub, it has slender, pendulous branches with an elegance lacking in the bushier forsythias, and in early and mid-spring they are laden

Euonymus fortunei 'Silver Queen'

MORE CLIMBERS AND WALL SHRUBS FOR CHALK *Abutilon megapotamicum* • *Actinidia* • *Akebia quinata* •

Forsythia suspensa

with golden yellow, bell-like flowers. Against a wall it will reach 4m (13ft). It needs a framework of wires to support it and tying in will be an annual job, but the effort will be well rewarded when the plant is in full bloom. (See Good Companions, page 87.)

For a slender plant with a strong structural appearance try the flannel bush, *Fremontodendron* 'California Glory'♥. This is a tall, evergreen wall shrub with rich egg-yellow flowers, each one 7cm (3in) wide. The flowers have no petals, only large, brightly coloured calyces. An improvement on the species *Fremontodendron californicum*, it was raised at Rancho Santa Ana Botanical Garden in California. Give it a sunny wall and it will soak up the warmth, growing to 5m (16ft) and producing flowers nonstop through the summer. The only word of caution is that it can cause skin and eye irritation and so is best placed away from areas where people might brush past it.

Another unusual shrub that loves warm, sunny walls and well-drained soil is the evergreen laburnum, *Piptanthus nepalensis*, from the Himalayas. The rich emerald, three-lobed foliage is semi-evergreen and contrasts well with the bright yellow, laburnum-like flowers produced in late spring. It is an elegant shrub, reaching 2.5m (8ft).

Fremontodendron 'California Glory'

Piptanthus nepalensis

Hedera helix • *Jasminum* • *Lonicera periclymenum* • *Schizophragma hydrangeoides* • *Solanum crispum* 'Glasnevin' •

COLOUR EFFECTS

Colour is a powerful element in garden design. Soft pastel shades create a gentle romantic feel, while rich, bold colours make gardens look vibrant and exciting. Light, too, as it changes from dawn to dusk and from day to day, has a significant effect on the garden picture; hazy early morning sun emphasizes texture, strong back light brings colours to life. The flowers and foliage of climbing plants bring colour to the garden at every level. Through careful selection, climbers can transform any ordinary planting scheme into something exceptional.

RIGHT: *Clematis* 'Kermesina'.

Green and white

Green is present in almost all gardens but is often overshadowed by showier colours. It is only when combined with white that green really moves to centre stage. Green symbolizes balance and harmony, while white represents purity and peace. Together they create a sense of calm and tranquillity – something that many yearn for in today's fast-paced world.

Ceanothus 'Popcorn'

GREEN AND WHITE FLOWERS

Ceanothus 'Popcorn' is a very useful evergreen wall shrub for a white garden. Instead of the usual fluffy blue ceanothus flowers, it has white ones, with rich toffee-brown centres. These appear in late spring and early summer on spiny branches that grow to 2.5m (8ft). Although the flowers do not inspire the same admiration as their blue relations, in a white planting scheme they are valuable for extending the period of interest of later-flowering climbers, such as the white form of *Cobaea scandens*♀ (cathedral bells).

   Clematis flowers provide wonderful bold forms that make a good contrast with sculptural green foliage. *Clematis* ALABAST ('Poulala')♀ has gorgeous white flowers, 15cm (6in) across, flushed with jade green. *Clematis* 'Gillian Blades'♀ is

Echo the colour of your planting with strong matching accessories. *Wisteria floribunda* 'Alba' is lovely on its own, but here its beauty is enhanced by an elegant white bench

Clematis ALABAST

OTHER WHITE-FLOWERED CLIMBERS AND WALL SHRUBS *Abutilon vitifolium* 'Veronica Tennant' •

one of the most beautiful of all clematis. It has very large, pure white flowers with distinctive curled and rippled edges to the sepals, making them appear thick and porcelain-like. The white anthers complete a stunning picture. It flowers from early to late summer, reaches 2.5m (8ft) and needs minimal attention.

Clematis 'John Huxtable'♔ is a late-flowering white, and a chance seedling from the pink *Clematis* 'Comtesse de Bouchaud'♔ (see page 136). Having the same free-flowering habit, shape and medium-sized flowers as its parent, it is a superb companion for climbing roses or for other clematis. It blooms from mid- to late summer, grows to 3m (10ft) and is a very good hybrid, useful for drawing the eye. (See Good Companions, page 96.)

Clematis 'Marie Boisselot'♔, also incorrectly called 'Madame le Coultre', is probably the best known of all the white hybrids. It has large, pure white flowers, 20cm (8in) across, with gold anthers; these are borne over a very long period, starting in late spring and repeating through the summer until at least mid-autumn, often later. With such a long season it also has longer growth, reaching 3.5m (12ft).

Clematis 'Mrs George Jackman'♔ is not as well known as *Clematis* 'Marie Boisselot', but it has a discreet charm and is an excellent choice for containers. Growing 2.5m (8ft) high, it produces elegant, semi-double, soft white flowers in early summer, followed by single blooms in mid- to late summer. The flowers have a cream bar when they first open and tan anthers, distinguishing them from the blooms of 'Marie Boisselot'.

Clematis 'Sylvia Denny', which reaches 2.5m (8ft) high, is a cross between *Clematis* 'Marie Boisselot' and the double white *Clematis* 'Duchess of Edinburgh' (see page 78). The semi-double, pure white flowers are smaller than those of the Duchess but are well formed and set off nicely by the bronze young foliage.

Clematis 'Gillian Blades'

Clematis 'Marie Boisselot'

Clematis 'John Huxtable'

Clematis 'Mrs George Jackman'

RESTRICTED COLOURS

The garden is no different from the painter's canvas in that the smaller the colour palette used, the more vital the individual components become. If you want to plant part of the garden entirely with white flowers, for example, think about using a mixture of forms and shapes: the long racemes of *Wisteria floribunda* 'Alba'♔ add strong vertical elements, while large clematis blooms give well-defined focal points. Richly textured flowers, such as camellias (here, *Camellia japonica* 'Silver Anniversary'), lend additional interest.

Carpenteria californica • *Dregea sinensis* • *Hydrangea anomala* subsp. *petiolaris* • *Jasminum officinale* • *Magnolia grandiflora* •

Rosa 'Adélaïde d'Orléans'

Rosa 'Albéric Barbier'

Rosa 'Bobbie James'

OTHER GOOD WHITE RAMBLING ROSES

Rosa MOUNTAIN SNOW ('Aussnow') Large, semi-double, white flowers with a light scent. Height 5m (16ft). Flowers in late spring and early summer.

Rosa 'Rambling Rector' ♔ (1) Semi-double, creamy-white, deliciously scented flowers. Height 7m (22ft). Flowers in late spring and early summer.

Rosa 'Sander's White Rambler' ♔ Semi-double, white flowers with a fresh fragrance. Height 6m (20ft). Flowers from early to midsummer.

Rosa SNOW GOOSE ('Auspom') White, pompon, scented flowers. Height 3.5m (12ft). Flowers in late spring and early summer, with additional blooms in midsummer.

Rosa 'Wedding Day' (2) Single, white flowers opening from apricot buds, with a strong fragrance. Height 10m (33ft). Flowers in late spring and early summer.

OTHER WHITE-FLOWERED CLIMBERS *Passiflora caerulea* 'White Lightning' • *Solanum laxum* 'Album' •

The semi-double blooms produced in early summer are followed by masses of singles in late summer.

There is a bewildering selection of white **rambler roses**. As young plants in the garden centre, many appear remarkably similar. Not only is there little difference in habit at this age, but the flowers pictured on the labels also look much the same. Homework is advisable as there can be a world of difference in the end result – and many are suitable only for huge spaces (see page 70). Ramblers bloom only once each year, between late spring and early summer, with a few exceptions that also produce scattered flowers later on.

Rosa 'Adélaïde d'Orléans'♀ is a good choice for a medium-sized garden. Although it reaches 5m (16ft), it has a delicate, pliable habit, making it ideal for pergolas. It is also almost evergreen and the small, white, semi-double flowers open showing the faintest hint of blush pink, with a delicate primrose scent.

Rosa 'Albéric Barbier'♀ grows vigorously to 6m (20ft) and has masses of virtually evergreen foliage. The main crop of creamy-white, fruit-scented flowers is borne in early summer and followed by an unusually respectable second crop in late summer. Its size and its strong, upright habit limit it to larger gardens, growing through trees and covering eyesores.

Rosa 'Bobbie James'♀ is one of the larger ramblers, reaching a bushy 10m (33ft). The creamy-white flowers are very fragrant and are produced in huge, heavy heads. It is ideal in large gardens, growing through trees, as the flower trusses will be in scale with the host.

Rosa filipes 'Kiftsgate'♀ is a stunning rose but is only suitable for gardens with a really huge space to fill. At Kiftsgate Court in the Cotswolds, where its growth is restricted by a beech hedge and a path, it fills an area of 25 by 30m (80 by 100ft) and has reached a height of 17m (56ft) – believed to be the largest rose in England. The creamy-white flowers have a sweet

Rosa filipes 'Kiftsgate'

Rosa 'Climbing Iceberg'

scent and are carried in enormous panicles from early to midsummer. A crop of oval hips in autumn is an added bonus.

For small gardens **climbing roses** make a better choice. They flower repeatedly through the summer and into early autumn, especially when fed generously, and build up a framework of flowering shoots that need only minor pruning.

Rosa 'Climbing Iceberg'♀ is a climbing sport of the bush rose *Rosa* 'Iceberg', and is identical in all but height, reaching 3.5m (12ft). It must not be hard pruned

otherwise it will revert to the bush form. The lightly scented, pure white flowers appear slightly translucent and are lovely grown with pale-coloured clematis. (See Good Companions, page 96.)

Rosa CRÈME DE LA CRÈME ('Gancre') has beautifully formed white buds opening to fragrant, creamy-white blooms. It grows to 3m (10ft) and has good, glossy, green foliage.

Rosa SWAN LAKE ('Macmed') is a bigger type, with large, blowsy, white flowers, with a pink flush in the middle,

Sollya heterophylla 'Alba' • *Stephanotis floribunda* • *Trachelospermum asiaticum* • *Wisteria brachybotrys* 'Shiro-kapitan' •

Trachelospermum jasminoides

ageing to off-white. The blooms are very pretty, but unfortunately not strongly scented. It grows to 4m (13ft).

Rosa 'White Cockade' is a very free-flowering rose, with hybrid tea flowers that have a gentle fragrance. It is a smaller grower, reaching just 2.5m (8ft), and is vigorous and healthy.

Trachelospermum jasminoides♔ is one of the best-scented white climbers. Surprisingly, this and its hardier relative *Trachelospermum asiaticum* (see pages 41, 81) are not widely grown. Perhaps it is because they are seen as being exotic and tender, and so are traditionally used as conservatory plants. They seem, however, to survive quite happily in temperate climates today in all but the coldest of winters. The thick, oval, evergreen foliage of *Trachelospermum jasminoides* is dark green and glossy, turning bronze in winter. All summer long it is covered with showers of sweetly scented, starry, white flowers that turn cream as they

age. Although it eventually reaches 7m (22ft), it grows relatively slowly and will not be difficult to control even if planted in a smaller space. *Trachelospermum jasminoides* 'Japonicum' has larger leaves, with downy undersides. It grows taller than the species, reaching 8m (26ft), and gives cover as effective as any ivy when mature.

GREEN AND WHITE FOLIAGE

Ivies (*Hedera*) dominate the foliage section, although there are many other choices, often grown for flowers, that also have good green or green and white foliage. Climbers such as the evergreen *Clematis armandii* (see page 119), with big bold foliage, and *Clematis cirrhosa* (see page 150), with pretty, fern-like leaves, give superb cover. It is worth taking a look at climbers out of season, even in winter, and assessing their foliage,

SCENT

Fragrance is a very strong ally in design. Along with colour and texture, it is the most atmospheric ingredient in gardens. Light, fruity scents make a garden lively and fresh, while rich, musky scents give a much more opulent feel. White flowers are among the most strongly perfumed, but many release their scent only at dusk, the white, often tubular or trumpet-shaped flowers (here, *Stephanotis floribunda*♔) designed to attract night-flying moths.

GOOD COMPANIONS

Extend the early flowering season of *Philadelphus coronarius* 'Variegatus'♔ (1) by growing the late-flowering *Clematis* 'John Huxtable'♔ (2) through it.

Trachelospermum jasminoides 'Variegatum'♔ (3) has variegated leaves but lacks flower power. The white *Rosa* 'Climbing Iceberg'♔ (4) boosts the flower colour without being too vigorous.

Clematis 'Early Sensation' (5) has dramatic silky white flowerheads, ideal for brightening up a plain green *Hedera helix* (6).

OTHER CLIMBERS WITH WHITE-VARIEGATED LEAVES *Actinidia kolomikta* • *Ceanothus* 'Pershore Zanzibar' •

Clematis armandii

Hedera helix 'Green Ripple'

Hedera helix 'Parsley Crested'

Trachelospermum jasminoides 'Variegatum'

or lack of it. In many cases, you see more of the foliage than the flowers.

Hedera helix 'Angularis', the Jersey ivy, also sometimes sold as 'Emerald Green' or 'Emerald Gem', has masses of soft, glossy, bright green leaves, more lush in appearance than the species. It is a vigorous ivy, reaching up to 7m (22ft), and is ideal for providing structure in the form of hedges or topiary shapes.

For smaller walls or for ground cover, *Hedera helix* 'Green Ripple' may be a better choice since it grows only to 2m (6ft). It has long, elegant, dark green leaves with grey veins, and in winter they take on an attractive copper hue. It is prone to produce plain green shoots over time and these should be cut back to the point at which they emerged. *Hedera helix* 'Parsley Crested'♡ ('Cristata'), of similar stature, is a classic choice when you need to add texture. The pale green leaves with their crimped and curled edges are reminiscent of parsley.

Creamy-white splashes and margins on the leaves of *Trachelospermum jasminoides* 'Variegatum'♡ make it useful for brightening up a dull spot. It is a very pretty plant, the foliage taking on crimson tones through winter. Add the richly fragrant, white flowers and compact height of just 4m (13ft) and it is a real star. (See Good Companions, left.) *Trachelospermum jasminoides* 'Wilsonii' has silver-veined green leaves.

WHAT CAUSES VARIEGATION?

Variation in leaf colour arises because of a lack of the green pigment chlorophyll in some of the plant cells. It is usually the result of a cell mutation, and can be inherited (genetic) or occur randomly (chimeric). If genetic, the colour change is stable, which means that if you propagate a green shoot on a plant with coloured leaves or sow seed from it, the colouring will reappear in the new plant. This applies both to green leaves with irregular markings (variegation), say in white or yellow, and to those of a single solid colour such as gold or purple.

A random mutation usually shows up as variegation. If you propagate from a green shoot or sow seed of the plant, the colour will not reoccur. This kind of variegation is the most common, but is often difficult to stabilize. Propagation must be from variegated or coloured shoots. In nature these forms usually die out, being weaker growers because of the lack of chlorophyll, which plants use to make the food they need for growth.

Variegation can also be the result of a viral infection, showing as discoloured veins or leaf areas. This form of variegation is relatively rare, but it is stable. *Lonicera japonica* 'Aureoreticulata' (see page 49) has this type of variegation, with golden yellow veins netting the leaves.

Clematis 'Warwickshire Rose' • *Cotoneaster atropurpureus* 'Variegatus' • *Jasminum officinale* 'Argenteovariegatum' •

Citrus shades

Yellow climbers and wall shrubs have a powerful effect in the garden. Although many people may wince at the mention of such a 'vulgar' colour, gardens that are disappointing are often so because yellow is absent. While the green of foliage is the perfect foil for reds and pinks, blues and purples need yellow to highlight them. Yellow and gold flowers and foliage are capable of lifting a planting scheme from the mundane to the sensational.

Yellow does not always mean strong, brazen colour. Soft, delicate tints, with white added, or rich, deep shades, with black added, are equally effective. Soft lemon works as well with purple, as does egg-yolk yellow or rich saffron yellow.

CITRUS FLOWERS

Acacia dealbata♀, the florist's mimosa, is a pure yellow and is a wonderful sight when trained against a warm, south-facing wall. Even without the stunning, fluffy, yellow balls of scented flowers that open in mid- and late winter, the evergreen, feathery, silver foliage is beautiful. This lovely wall shrub can grow

Acacia dealbata

rather large, to 7.5m (25ft) if untrimmed; cut it back to a framework after flowering and it can be kept to 4m (13ft).

It is hardier than generally thought, but can be badly damaged in extremely cold winters. The growth is so rapid, however, that the plant soon regenerates. It dislikes chalky or limy soil, and needs protection from strong winds.

Acacia dealbata 'Gaulois Astier' makes a much smaller, bushier plant of 4m (13ft) and is becoming more widely available. Plenty of sun is essential for the wood to ripen fully and produce a good crop of flowers the following year.

Acacia longifolia, the Sydney golden wattle, is a more lime-tolerant species. The blue-green evergreen leaves are in fact modified leaf-stalks (phyllodes), but perform all the usual leaf functions. It flowers in early spring, in long, feathery, yellow spikes, and grows to 6m (20ft).

Another wall shrub with similar flowers of fluffy stamens without petals is **Azara serrata**♀. It bears its blooms in late spring and early summer, among the mid-green evergreen leaves, and reaches 4m (13ft). It is best in a sheltered spot away from cold winds. If pruning is needed, cut back immediately after flowering.

The soft primrose blooms of *Rosa banksiae* 'Lutea' and the fresh young growth of *Hedera colchica* 'Dentata Variegata' bring alive the beautiful flowers of *Wisteria sinensis*.

Azara serrata

Jasminum humile 'Revolutum'

Cytisus battandieri 'Yellow Tail'

Jasminum nudiflorum

The exotic-looking pineapple broom, **Cytisus battandieri**♥, has laburnum-like, evergreen leaves with a silky, silvery sheen. The pineapple-scented, bright yellow flowers are packed onto erect racemes 10cm (4in) long, produced in early and midsummer. Introduced from Morocco, it loves a hot, dry, sunny spot and needs a wall to give of its best. It is a big shrub, reaching 4m (13ft), and is very hardy. **Cytisus battandieri 'Yellow Tail'**♥ is an improved form, with 15cm (6in) flower spikes.

An exotic wall shrub for a sunny spot, the flannel bush, **Fremontodendron 'California Glory'**♥ (see page 89), has stunning saucer-shaped, waxy, egg-yellow flowers. They are produced all summer long on a plant 5m (16ft) tall.

Jasminum humile 'Revolutum'♥ is a beautiful jasmine. Its rich, dark, semi-evergreen leaves make a perfect setting for the deep yellow, slightly scented flowers, borne from early spring to late autumn. A scrambling shrub, 2.5m (8ft) tall, it loves a warm, sunny wall; it does not thrive in very cold climates.

If you live in a cold area or have poor soil, choose the wall shrub **Jasminum nudiflorum**♥ instead. This is the winter jasmine, which flowers from late autumn to early spring, before the leaves appear. It is not a neat grower, having awkward angular branches to 4.5m (15ft), but this

Rosa THE PILGRIM

Rosa xanthina 'Canary Bird'

is forgiven for the mass of brilliant yellow flowers it produces. To prevent the build-up of dead wood, prune immediately after flowering. It is well suited to making an informal hedge when trained along a low post-and-wire framework.

Yellow **roses** are often neglected in favour of their pink relations but there are some good healthy roses with fabulous yellow flowers (see also pages 130–31). *Rosa* 'Alchymist' blooms only in early summer but the flowers are gorgeous. Strongly scented with an old-fashioned shape, they are rich golden yellow flushed with orange. It grows to 4m (13ft).

Rosa THE PILGRIM ('Auswalker') is a beautiful shade of delicate yellow fading to white at the edges. It is one of the best of the English roses, making a superb climber and reaching 3m (10ft) against a wall. The fragrant, rosette-shaped flowers are produced all summer.

Rosa xanthina 'Canary Bird'♔ is not usually seen as a climber, but does make a very effective wall shrub. The musk-scented flowers are single and small, just 5cm (2in) across, and appear in early spring – among the first roses of the year.

THE SUN KING STORY

The most exciting new plants are often discovered by accident. *Sophora* SUN KING ('Hilsop')♔ was found as a rogue seedling in a batch of *Nothofagus* (southern beech) sent from Chile to Hillier Nurseries. No one knew what it was, but luckily it was put to one side to be identified. It was planted in the early 1980s in the Sir Harold Hillier Gardens in Hampshire in an area known as The Pond, a frost pocket in heavy clay soil.

Despite the waterlogging and cold in winter and baked soil in summer, the plant thrived, producing stunning golden flowers. Launched in 1998, it won numerous accolades and many thousands of plants have since been sold.

Sophora SUN KING

There may be a few bonus flowers in mid- to late summer. Easy and trouble-free, it grows to 3m (10ft).

The evergreen, pinnate foliage of *Sophora* SUN KING ('Hilsop')♔ is deep emerald green, which makes a stunning contrast to the clusters of rich yellow, bell-like flowers that appear in late winter and early spring. Against a wall this shrub grows more vigorously than when in open ground and may reach 6m (20ft), but can easily be trained to a smaller framework.

CITRUS FOLIAGE

Yellow and gold attract the eye and can be used to create illusions in gardens, perhaps drawing attention from a less attractive area, or giving the impression of greater space. A long, narrow site can be made more interesting by putting a trellis screen across at the halfway point. When this is planted with a yellow- or gold-leaved climber, the eye will go straight to it, only later on seeing what may be beyond.

MORE GOOD YELLOW-FLOWERED CLIMBERS AND WALL SHRUBS *Abutilon* 'John Thompson' •

Hedera colchica 'Sulphur Heart'

Hedera helix 'Goldchild'

Hedera helix 'Goldheart'

Hedera helix 'Buttercup'

> ### KEEPING 'GOLDHEART' GOLD
>
> As with many variegated plants, *Hedera helix* 'Goldheart' occasionally produces plain green shoots. These should be removed as they are seen, cutting right back to the point where they join the main stem.
> Do not use 'Goldheart' for ground cover since, unusually for an ivy, shoots growing on the ground lose their variegation.

Ivy is ideal for this kind of screen. Its self-clinging growth is evergreen and vigorous, but not rampant, and there is a huge range of varieties available (see pages 152–53). One of the very best is *Hedera colchica* 'Sulphur Heart'♀. This is an extremely hardy, large-leaved ivy, growing to 10m (33ft). The slightly waved leaves are dark green splashed with yellow and pale green; occasionally a leaf may be entirely yellow. It makes a very impressive sight threaded in and out of large-squared trellis.

The fabulous golden yellow of *Hedera helix* 'Buttercup' is unique. The leaves are medium sized and a rich buttery gold. The colour fades very slowly through lemon yellow to soft green. In full sun it can scorch a little and is best on semi-shaded walls. Grow it on its own or with other climbers; either way it performs well and reaches a height of 2m (6ft). (See Good Companions, page 102.)

'Buttercup' is one of the few coloured ivies that come true from seed. This is because the colour is a result of a true

genetic mutation. If you are taking a cutting, choose a light green shoot since this will propagate more easily; the colour will come true as the plant grows.

Hedera helix 'Goldchild'♀ is a smaller-leaved, less hardy ivy. The foliage is bright green, with pale green in the centre and a golden yellow margin; with age it takes on a more blue-green and creamy-yellow appearance. This is a bright, attractive plant, growing to 1.2m (4ft), but it is not suitable for colder areas.

Hedera helix 'Goldheart', now officially known as *Hedera helix* 'Oro di Bogliasco', is quite distinctive. The stems have a pinkish-red colouring, contrasting with the small, deep green leaves with rich golden yellow centres. It is especially

Campsis radicans f. *flava* • *Clematis tangutica* • *Coronilla valentina* subsp. *glauca* • *Genista* 'Porlock' •

Humulus lupulus 'Aureus'

GETTING THE BEST FROM HUMULUS

When buying a *Humulus lupulus* cultivar, be sure to choose a female clone, so that it will bear fruit.

Wear long sleeves and gloves when handling the plant to avoid scratches caused by the hairy shoots.

Plant it 2m (6ft) away from where you want it to appear and lead the younger foliage into the prime spot. This will ensure that the oldest foliage, and the insect damage invariably found on it, will be hidden.

Place the base away from other plants so that the inevitable suckers are easy to deal with.

Train new shoots in regularly so that the plant ends up where you want it.

Grow it on a feature that is attractive in its own right so that the plant's herbaceous nature is not an issue.

good for brightening up a shady wall. With a height of just 1.2m (4ft), it is an excellent choice where space is limited.

If space is not a problem, and bold, dramatic colour is called for then try **Humulus lupulus 'Aureus'**♀ (golden hop), a twining, herbaceous climber that loves sun, grows to 6m (20ft) and will cover a large wall or pergola with ease. It has a wonderful cottage-garden feel, mixing well with roses and clematis. The foliage is bright golden yellow and the hanging clusters of flowers, borne in mid- to late summer, are light green and conical, expanding in autumn into the fruit known as hops. (See Good Companions, right.) **'Golden Tassels'** is more compact, growing to just 3m (10ft).

Jasmine is a vital ingredient of summer and there are two lovely twining, golden-leaved, deciduous varieties. Don't choose these if you want masses of richly scented blooms, because the leaf colour seems to be produced at the expense of flowers. Expect a handful of richly scented, white

GOOD COMPANIONS

Plant a carpet of blue *Muscari armeniacum*♀ (1) at the foot of the golden yellow ivy *Hedera helix* 'Buttercup' (2) for a strong spring colour scheme.

Lavandula stoechas subsp. *stoechas* f. *leucantha* 'Purple Wings' (3) sits well at the foot of *Jasminum officinale* FIONA SUNRISE ('Frojas') (4), both revelling in the same soil conditions.

Humulus lupulus 'Aureus'♀ (5) makes a genial host for the vigorous, late-flowering *Clematis* 'Etoile Violette'♀ (6), the golden foliage setting off the rich purple clematis flowers.

MORE YELLOW-LEAVED CLIMBERS *Hedera helix* 'Angularis Aurea' • *Hedera helix* 'Midas Touch' •

flowers from midsummer to early autumn. *Jasminum officinale* 'Aureum' is very effective, growing to 4m (13ft), with yellow-variegated green leaves. Even more dramatic is *Jasminum officinale* FIONA SUNRISE ('Frojas'), a plant that was discovered simultaneously in two different gardens, hence its somewhat hybrid name. It has rich yellow foliage, best in a slightly shaded position, and it is a neat, compact grower, reaching 2–4m (6–13ft). It makes an ideal plant for the pillars of a pergola or for growing up one side of an arch. (See Good Companions, opposite.)

The evergreen twining climber *Trachelospermum asiaticum* 'Golden Memories' is a new introduction. It has glossy, golden leaves and, in summer, fragrant, creamy-white flowers that fade to cream. As with the jasmines, the flowers are not profusely borne. Altogether daintier than the species (see page 41), it grows to 3m (10ft).

Trachelospermum asiaticum 'Golden Memories'

PROTECTING GOLDEN-LEAVED CLIMBERS

The lack of chlorophyll in golden-leaved climbers means that the foliage is more sensitive to sun and many are prone to scorching. If given too much shade, however, the golden colour will often disappear, leaving the leaves a soft green. The best compromise is to plant such climbers on a semi-shaded wall, where they will be out of the sun in the hottest part of the day.

Jasminum officinale FIONA SUNRISE has pretty, golden, pinnate leaves and provides background colour all season long, making a strong foil for flowering plants such as *Spiraea japonica* 'Dart's Red'.

103

Kadsura japonica 'Variegata' • *Lonicera japonica* 'Aureoreticulata' • *Solanum laxum* 'Album Variegatum' •

Plum, purple and red

Plum, purple and red are fabulously evocative colours in the garden. They suggest richness and warmth and give great visual depth to planting. Climbers with flowers or foliage of these shades mix exceptionally well with other colours, but should not be used too freely as background plants because the darker shades tend to recede. They are best used as occasional anchor plants or to provide glamorous highlights for other climbers.

Clematis 'Romantika' drips with sensational inky-purple flowers, an ideal companion for a pale climbing rose.

PLUM, PURPLE AND RED FLOWERS

Akebia quinata, also known as the chocolate vine, has five-lobed, cocoa-scented flowers, which may be any colour ranging from dark purple to cream; at its best it is a delicious rich plum. Given its variability, it is safest to buy the plant when it is in bloom so that you can be sure about the colour. Cream and light mauve cultivars have been selected (see page 50), and might be useful if you have a lighter colour scheme. The scent is also worth checking since it can be rich and spicy or all but absent. *Akebia quinata* is a desirable climber for larger gardens. Be prepared to give it plenty of space: it will need around 10m (33ft). The handsome, semi-evergreen, choisya-like foliage means the plant looks pleasing even when not in flower. Greyish-violet or purplish, sausage-shaped seedpods, containing black seeds in a white pulp, sometimes follow the flowers.

Spectacular red flowers are a feature of the shrubby bottlebrush, *Callistemon citrinus* 'Splendens' ♀. The branches are lined with lance-shaped, green leaves; young shoots are silky and coloured soft pink. The bottlebrush flowers are carried at the ends of the shoots in spring and summer. Callistemon needs regular pruning to prevent it getting leggy. Cut off the flowerheads as they begin to fade to make the stems bushier, and train the shoots into a fan shape. Against a wall, it can grow up to 8m (26ft), but

Akebia quinata

Callistemon citrinus 'Splendens'

MORE PURPLE AND RED CLIMBERS *Ampelopsis brevipedunculata* • *Berberidopsis corallina* • *Billardiera longiflora* •

regular pruning can keep it to a more manageable 5m (16ft).

Clematis abound with rich colours, introduced through the red American *Clematis texensis* and the purple European species *Clematis viticella* (see pages 138–139*)*. *Clematis* 'Allanah', up to 3m (10ft) high, is a deep bright red with black anthers. The flowers, with widely spaced sepals, are extremely attractive and are produced at the ends of the stems from early summer to early autumn.

Clematis 'Crimson King' is an old variety, 3m (10ft) tall, sometimes known incorrectly in North America as 'Crimson Star'. It carries its flowers very elegantly, holding them out in a horizontal manner something like a waterlily. Produced from mid- to late summer, the flowers are crimson with light brown anthers; most are single, but some are semi-double.

Clematis 'Allanah'

Clematis 'Ernest Markham'

Clematis 'Ernest Markham'♀ is a lovely, glowing petunia-red with a velvety texture and light brown anthers. It needs sun to flower well and blooms from midsummer to mid-autumn. At 4m (13ft) tall, it is much larger than most.

OTHER GOOD PLUM, PURPLE AND RED CLEMATIS

Clematis 'Edomurasaki' Deep purple-blue with red anthers; mid- to late summer. Height 3m (10ft).

Clematis 'Etoile de Malicorne' Rich purplish blue with a darker bar and deep wine anthers; midsummer to early autumn. Height 3m (10ft).

Clematis 'Madame Edouard André' Rich crimson, cupped sepals with a darker bar and pale yellow anthers; mid- to late summer. Height 2.5m (8ft).

Clematis 'Madame Grangé'♀ (1) Deep purplish red with reddish-purple anthers and distinctive curling sepals; midsummer to early autumn. Height 3m (10ft).

Clematis 'Rouge Cardinal' Velvety crimson with auburn-red anthers; midsummer to early autumn. Height 3m (10ft).

Clematis 'Warszawska Nike'♀ (2) Deep, velvety purple with bright gold anthers; midsummer to early autumn. Height 3m (10ft).

Clematis 'Westerplatte' (3) Very rich purple-red with darker anthers; early summer to early autumn. Height 2.5m (8ft).

Clematis 'Gipsy Queen'

Clematis 'Romantika' is an exceptionally beautiful clematis. The deep inky-purple flowers are quite distinctive and a must for growing through either a pale rose, such as *Rosa* 'New Dawn'♀ (see page 130), or a light foliage shrub such as *Cotinus coggygria* GOLDEN SPIRIT ('Ancot'). The flowers appear from midsummer to early autumn, on a plant 2–2.5m (6–8ft) high.

Clematis 'Gipsy Queen'♀ is a lovely cultivar from the golden days of clematis breeding in the 1870s and has stood the test of time. Its rich, velvety violet-purple flowers, with claret anthers, are carried in large numbers from early summer right through to early autumn. It is vigorous, reaching 3m (10ft), and combines wonderfully with old roses. (See also page 67.)

Bougainvillea × *buttiana* 'Mrs Butt' • *Clematis* 'Gravetye Beauty' • *Clematis* 'Purple Spider' • *Clematis* 'Ville de Lyon' •

Clematis 'Jackmannii Superba'

Clematis ROSEMOOR

Clematis 'Niobe'

Clematis VICTOR HUGO

Clematis 'Kermesina'

Clematis **'Jackmannii Superba'** is another strong old hybrid with large, broad, violet-purple sepals and creamy-lime anthers. It is, however, difficult to propagate and 'Gipsy Queen' is sometimes sold under its name, although this is easily distinguished because of its dark red anthers. If you buy it from a reputable nursery this issue will not arise. The flowers are produced from midsummer to early autumn and are almost square in shape. In average growing conditions it will reach 2.5m (8ft), but with lots of feed and good soil it will grow to 4m (13ft).

Clematis **'Niobe'**♛ is the best-known red. The flowers are deepest red with an almost black tint when they open, fading slightly with age, and with contrasting yellow anthers. In hot climates the flower colour is even deeper. 'Niobe' is excellent either in the ground or in pots, grows to 2.5–3m (8–10ft) and flowers from late spring through to early autumn.

Clematis ROSEMOOR **('Evipo002')** is one of a quartet of clematis named after the Royal Horticultural Society's four gardens to celebrate the society's bicentenary in 2004. Growing to 3m (10ft), it bears velvety red blooms with cream anthers, from early summer to early autumn. (See also page 17.)

Clematis VICTOR HUGO **('Evipo007')** has widely spaced, dark blue-purple sepals and dark violet anthers. The flowers are borne from early summer to early autumn. It grows to 3m (10ft) and prefers full sun. (See Good Companions, page 109.)

Clematis VINO **('Poulvo')** starts to flower earlier than most dark red clematis, producing large, single, purple-red blooms with yellow anthers from late spring to late summer. It reaches 2.5m (8ft).

The flowers of *Clematis* **'Viola'** are almost square, and a deep bluish-violet colour with greenish-yellow anthers. They are borne from early summer to late summer, on a plant up to 3m (10ft) tall.

For coastal sites *Clematis* **'Voluceau'** is an excellent choice. It has twisted, petunia-red flowers, 15cm (6in) wide, with yellow stamens. It is very strong-growing, up to 3m (10ft), and blooms all summer. Very dark clematis such as this are best seen against a light background. They work especially well growing through variegated ivies (see pages 152–53) and *Trachelospermum jasminoides* 'Variegatum'♛ (see page 97).

Clematis *viticella* has contributed some superb richly coloured hybrids. *Clematis* **'Kermesina'**♛ is a fabulous free-flowering cultivar with intensely red flowers and black anthers. It often has a green flush to the tips early in the season, which disappears later in the summer. Like most viticellas, it flowers from midsummer to early autumn and grows to 3m (10ft).

MORE PURPLE AND RED CLIMBERS *Cobaea scandens* • *Hedera helix* 'Atropurpurea' • *Lathyrus odoratus* 'Cupani' •

Clematis 'Purpurea Plena Elegans'♀ may be a wild seedling from *Clematis viticella*. Mentioned in gardening books as far back as the 16th century, it was a great favourite in Elizabethan gardens. Growing to 3.5m (12ft) high, it has small, double, violet-purple flowers with a red flush through the sepals. The flowers hang down slightly and are best viewed from the same level or below. It is especially good threaded through other climbers as its foliage is not too heavy. (See page 26 and see Good Companions, page 109.)

Another double-flowered form is officially known as **Clematis viticella 'Flore Pleno'** but is most often sold as 'Mary Rose'. It is difficult to find in nurseries but is worth the hunt because of its soft, smoky amethyst flowers, which combine extremely tastefully with many other shades. Its subtle colouring is best appreciated in a position where it gets late afternoon sun. It is 3m (10ft) high.

Clematis 'Royal Velours'♀ is a very old, viticella-type hybrid, raised in France, with deep, satin-purple flowers and green-black anthers. Like many of the French hybrids it is tough and free-flowering. It grows to 3m (10ft) in height.

Clematis 'Purpurea Plena Elegans'

APHIDS

The term aphids applies to sap-sucking insects of all colours, although greenfly and blackfly are most familiar. Telltale signs are distorted shoots and a black sooty growth on the leaves. The aphids suck the sap of their hosts, often transmitting viral diseases in the process. They also exude a sugary substance called honeydew, which encourages sooty mould.

Treatment with insecticide is very effective, as is biological control. Initial infestation usually occurs as the plant starts into growth. Careful observation and timely intervention – removing the aphids as soon as they are seen – can nip infestations in the bud.

Crinodendron hookerianum♀ looks decidedly exotic, with red, lantern-shaped flowers hanging beneath dark green, lance-shaped leaves. A native of Chile, it is best in a sheltered site, where it can grow to 4–10m (13–33ft) depending on the amount of protection. It needs an acid soil and a position away from strong sun and winds, which may scorch the leaves. There are many 'exotic' wall shrubs that do not live up to their descriptions; this is not one of them. It performs reliably and the branches drip with fabulous flowers. The late Sir Harold Hillier described it as 'one of the gems of the garden'.

Lonicera × *brownii* 'Dropmore Scarlet', the scarlet-trumpet honeysuckle, should be a triumph of colour and fragrance, but disappointingly it has somewhat tomato-red flowers and no scent. Add to this its susceptibility to aphid attack and, despite the huge numbers sold each year, it is not the best choice for gardens. On the positive side, it has semi-evergreen foliage, grows to 4m (13ft) and produces flowers for a long period from midsummer to mid-autumn. There is also another cultivar called *Lonicera* × *brownii* 'Fuchsioides' that is almost identical.

Lonicera periclymenum 'Serotina'♀, the late Dutch or late red honeysuckle, is a real gem. The whorls of creamy, tubular flowers are similar to those of the species, but with a rich red flush on the outside, and they are produced later in the season,

Clematis 'Royal Velours'

from midsummer through to mid-autumn. This is a gorgeous deciduous climber with richly scented flowers and foliage with a dark, slightly blue-purple tone. It grows to 7m (22ft) and loves dappled shade with a cool root run. (See Good companions, page 109 and see page 129.)

Lonicera × *brownii* 'Dropmore Scarlet'

A tender, twining, herbaceous climber from Mexico, *Rhodochiton atrosanguineus*♀ is an ideal plant for a conservatory; if grown in a container, it can be brought out into the garden during the summer. The purplish-red, tubular flowers are intriguing, each one hanging from a purple-black, bell-shaped calyx. They are produced non-stop all summer long among heart-shaped foliage, on a slim plant of just 3m (10ft) tall, and are followed by shiny, plum-coloured seedpods.

Ribes speciosum

Ribes speciosum♀ is a good choice if you like the unusual. It is semi-evergreen with arching, bristly, currant-like branches that, in mid- and late spring, bear clusters of pendent, fuchsia-like, rich red flowers all along their length. Growing to 3m (10ft) against a wall, it is best trained formally so the flowers can be appreciated. In colder areas it will need the shelter of a warm wall to be at its best.

Roses add opulence to planting schemes but do check for fragrance before buying. Most red climbing roses are climbing sports of hybrid tea roses and are hence identical in form to their non-climbing parent. *Rosa* 'Climbing Ena Harkness' has rich red, strongly fragrant and slightly hanging blooms, showing

Rosa 'Climbing Etoile de Hollande'

wonderfully on a high wall mixed with rich purple clematis. It grows to 5m (16ft) and blooms from early to late summer, with a few bonus flowers later on.

Rosa 'Climbing Etoile de Hollande'♀ is a vigorous grower, reaching 6m (20ft). Its beautiful, deep crimson flowers with a wonderful old rose fragrance appear from early to midsummer, with another good flush in late summer. A little larger than *Rosa* 'Climbing Ena Harkness', it holds its flowers in a more upright manner, giving it a bolder, more formal appearance.

Rosa 'Guinée'

Rosa 'Guinée' is probably the darkest of all the red climbers. It has fabulous, richly perfumed flowers, up to 10cm (4in) across, which are borne in summer. That said, it is also a relatively difficult rose to grow, as it requires good soil and regular feeding. Growing to 5m (16ft), it looks wonderful if you can give it sufficient attention, even doing well in shade; but without pampering it very often fizzles out and dies. Plant this rose in spring rather than in autumn to give it the best chance of success.

OTHER GOOD PLUM, PURPLE AND RED ROSES

Rosa ALTISSIMO ('Delmur') (**1**) Lightly scented climbing rose with long-lasting, single or semi-double, deep blood-red flowers flushed with crimson, borne in early and late summer. Rich dark foliage. Grows to 2.5m (8ft).

Rosa 'Bleu Magenta'♀ (**2**) Nearly thornless rambler with very double, crimson flowers, ageing through purple-violet to slate blue, borne in early summer. Lightly scented. Grows to 4m (13ft).

Rosa DUBLIN BAY ('Macdub')♀ Climber with shallow, rounded, rich crimson flowers carried among lustrous foliage from summer to autumn. Lightly scented. Healthy. Only 2.5m (8ft) high.

MORE PURPLE AND RED WALL SHRUBS *Abutilon* 'Kentish Belle' • *Camellia japonica* 'Adolphe Audusson' •

Rosa TESS OF THE D'URBERVILLES

Vitis coignetiae CLARET CLOAK

The David Austin English roses make lovely climbers for shorter walls, reaching around 3m (10ft) when mature. Very free-flowering and disease-resistant, and needing minimal attention, they are the ideal roses for busy gardeners. *Rosa* TESS OF THE D'URBERVILLES ('Ausmove') has strongly scented, rich red flowers borne all through the summer and autumn until leaf fall. (See Good Companions, below.)

PLUM, PURPLE AND RED FOLIAGE

Plum, purple and red foliage is rare in climbers. *Vitis coignetiae* CLARET CLOAK ('Frovit') is a form of the giant-leaved vine, with rich purple-red young shoots, maturing to dark olive-green as they age. The bold colour returns with vivid scarlet and crimson autumn

Vitis vinifera 'Purpurea'

GOOD COMPANIONS

The velvet flowers of *Clematis* VICTOR HUGO ('Evipo007') (1) are so dark that they need a light background to show them off properly; *Philadelphus coronarius* 'Aureus' ♛ (2) fits the bill perfectly.

Clematis 'Purpurea Plena Elegans' ♛ (3) threads its way through *Vitis vinifera* 'Purpurea' ♛ (4), providing the spectacular flowers that the vine lacks.

For a cottage-garden look, *Lonicera periclymenum* 'Serotina' ♛ (5) is the perfect partner for *Rosa* TESS OF THE D'URBERVILLES ('Ausmove') (6). They bloom together, giving a fanfare of colour and perfume.

tones before the leaves fall. It has bloomy purple, grape-like fruit in late summer. A vigorous, tendril climber, it needs at least 5m (16ft) to spread out fully, and will appreciate a moist root run.

Vitis vinifera 'Purpurea' ♛ is the best-known purple-leaved climber. It is planted a great deal in gardens, as it has claret-red leaves that hold their colour all season and mature to a deep wine purple. It grows to 7m (22ft) and produces small, dark purple fruit. It is hardy, easy to grow and makes a fantastic host for all types of other climbers. It also associates especially well with silver-foliage plants. (See Good Companions, left, and see page 22.)

109

Chaenomeles × *superba* 'Crimson and Gold' • *Clianthus puniceus* • *Cotoneaster horizontalis* • *Pyracantha* 'Mohave' •

Blue and silver

Blue is the most sought-after colour: gardeners tend to gravitate to its soothing tones even without thinking. Silver is a light and exciting foil to blue and to all the other colours in the spectrum. Both blue and silver have the same neutral quality in gardens, and can act as a transitional colour between more strident hues.

Clematis 'Daniel Deronda'

Clematis 'Fuji-musume'

Clematis 'Ken Donson'

Large-flowered clematis are an especially useful group of climbers having many superb blue varieties, such as the late-flowering *Clematis* 'Perle d'Azur' (see Late summer).

BLUE FLOWERS

Clematis hybrids provide a wide range of blue flowers but often they contain more than a hint of purple. Those described below reach a height of about 3m (10ft), unless stated otherwise.

Clematis 'Daniel Deronda'♀ has large, violet-blue flowers and creamy anthers. Semi-double and single flowers are produced in early summer, with smaller, single blooms over a long period from midsummer to early autumn.

Clematis 'Fuji-musume'♀ has to be one of the best clematis ever produced,

with perfectly formed flowers, 12cm (5in) across, in a delicious shade of sky blue, profusely borne on a neat, compact plant, 2.5m (8ft) tall. It blooms first in late spring to early summer, and again in late summer to early autumn. This cultivar will probably always be scarce because it is hard to propagate, flowering so freely that it produces very little material suitable for cuttings.

Clematis 'Haku-okan' is a rich purple-blue with a prominent boss of creamy-white stamens, prompting its Japanese name, which means white royal crown. It is exceptionally free-flowering once

established, but can take a little while to get going. Flowers are produced from late spring to early summer and then again in late summer.

Clematis 'Ken Donson'♀ has handsome, well-shaped, deep blue flowers with golden anthers. They are borne from late spring to early summer, with a second crop in late summer. It mixes well with deciduous shrubs like the black elder *Sambucus nigra* 'Eva' (formerly known as 'Black Lace').

Ceanothus

Stunning, fluffy, usually blue flowers make *Ceanothus* or California lilacs some of our most popular wall shrubs. They have a bushy, angular habit of growth, with small, oval, grooved leaves, which may be evergreen or deciduous. They flower either in spring or late summer. They all grow quickly and flower well when young, making them an excellent choice for bringing maturity to new gardens or for revitalizing older ones.

Ceanothus are native to large parts of the Pacific coast of North America, flourishing on sandy, acid soil in hot sun. In cooler climates, they need the warmth of a wall, a sunny spot and well-drained soil to be at their best.

The species are hardier than the hybrids and prefer a poorer soil. The hybrids need a rich soil, with more humus, but it should still be well drained. They will tolerate some lime, but do not thrive on very shallow soils over chalk. All are very happy in seaside gardens, standing up well to salt-laden winds.

Pruning, if needed to keep growth within bounds, should be done immediately after flowering for evergreens, preferably from a young age, and in late

Ceanothus 'Concha'♔ is evergreen, with dark, glossy leaves and rich, deep blue flowers opening from distinctive reddish buds in late spring. The branches are arching and the plant grows to 5m (16ft) in height. This is an excellent hybrid, which makes a fine host for many climbers.

winter for deciduous cultivars. The heights given here are for plants grown as wall shrubs, and would be less for plants grown in open ground. (See also pages 56, 72–73, 86–87, 92 and 135.)

OTHER GOOD CEANOTHUS

Ceanothus 'Cascade'♔ Masses of powder-blue flowers from spring to early summer. Evergreen and vigorous, to 6m (20ft), with a loose habit.

Ceanothus 'Dark Star'♔ Honey-scented, deep purplish-blue flowers in clusters in early spring. Evergreen. Grows to 4m (13ft).

Ceanothus × *delileanus* 'Henri Desfossé' Large, deep violet-blue flowers throughout summer. Semi-evergreen, losing its foliage in colder areas. Height 3m (10ft).

Ceanothus 'Italian Skies'♔ Bright blue flowers in late spring. Evergreen. Slightly tender and best in a sheltered spot. Grows to 3m (10ft).

Ceanothus 'Blue Mound'♔ (1) makes a large, solid, evergreen mound, 4m (13ft) high, with dark green leaves. Dense clusters of bright blue flowers with a hint of violet are freely produced in late spring. It is a wide-spreading plant and so makes a good choice where there is border space in front of a wall.

Ceanothus griseus var. *horizontalis* 'Yankee Point' is really a low-growing ground-cover shrub but when it is trained against a wall it reaches a height of 3m (10ft) and waterfalls beautifully. The evergreen leaves are the perfect complement for the brilliant blue flowers in late spring and early summer.

Ceanothus 'Puget Blue'♔ (2) is a tough and hardy form of the evergreen *Ceanothus impressus* (Santa Barbara ceanothus), and a good choice for

colder areas. Dark blue flowers are freely produced in mid- and late spring. Against a wall, it will reach up to 5m (16ft).

Clematis 'Kiri Te Kanawa'

Ipomoea tricolor 'Heavenly Blue'

Clematis 'Lord Nevill'

Plumbago auriculata

Clematis 'Lord Nevill' has elegant, ruffled flowers in deep blue with darker veins and deep red anthers; they are produced from late spring to early summer, with a second crop in late summer. An older variety that is not widely grown, it sits very well with other garden plants.

The morning glory Ipomoea tricolor 'Heavenly Blue' is one of the most stunning blue-flowered climbers. A twining, tender annual that clings on to any form of support, it provides quick cover and is delightful combined with bedding plants in the summer. The flowers are produced continuously from summer to early autumn on a plant that grows to 3–4m (10–13ft) tall.

Passiflora caerulea♀, or blue passion flower (see page 141), adds a wonderful exotic feel to patio areas with its amazing white flowers with violet-blue crowns. The flowers are carried from early summer right through to late autumn and are often followed by orange fruit. The plant is evergreen, climbs with tendrils and grows to 10m (33ft).

The blue plumbago, Plumbago auriculata♀ (Plumbago capensis), is used in hotter climates as a hedging shrub but in temperate regions it has to be confined to a conservatory in all but the most sheltered gardens. Clusters of sky-blue, primrose-shaped flowers are produced on the new growth from summer until early winter. It is evergreen and fast-growing, reaching an ultimate height of 6m (20ft).

For an unusual blue climbing plant try Sollya heterophylla♀, the bluebell

If double-flowered divas are wanted, then Clematis 'Kiri Te Kanawa' should be first in line. It produces large, fabulously double, rich blue flowers all through the season, first from late spring to early summer and again from late summer to early autumn. This is a good plant for a container. (See Good Companions, right.)

Clematis 'Lady Betty Balfour' is a superb, deep, velvety purple-blue with

yellow anthers. It is a strong grower, reaching 3.5m (12ft), but it flowers late, from early to mid-autumn. It needs a sunny position to ripen the growth sufficiently to survive the winter and start the flowering period a little earlier the following year. This clematis has been used extensively in breeding programmes to try to bring the deep blue gene to new varieties.

USING BLUE IN SUN AND SHADE

Blue is at its best in shade, gaining a special luminosity – just think of a bluebell wood. This enables it to be planted with any other colour in shade. In a sunny site, blue looks at its best with other colours that have blue in their make up, such as mauve or pink.

BLUE AND RED

Planting schemes with lots of blue and red together are best avoided as these colours are at opposite ends of the spectrum. Because blue has a very short wavelength and red a very long one, the eye has to work hard to focus on the two and therefore becomes tired very quickly.

OTHER CLIMBERS AND WALL SHRUBS WITH BLUE & SILVER LEAVES Acacia dealbata • Buddleja crispa •

Sollya heterophylla

BLUE AND SILVER FOLIAGE

Blue and silver foliage is very rare in climbing plants. Some acacias have fantastic silver foliage (see page 98), and the Cootamundra wattle, *Acacia baileyana* '**Purpurea**'☙, is particularly spectacular. Sometimes grown as a large shrub or small tree, it is more often trained on a framework to cover a wall. The graceful, feathery, evergreen leaves, beautiful deep purple when young, mature to a lovely silvery grey. The plant needs a fertile, well-drained site in full sun and a frost-free position, where it will eventually reach 3m (10ft).

Ivies (*Hedera*) provide good silvery foliage to contrast with the flowers of other plants. *Hedera helix* '**Adam**' has rather small green leaves with grey-green centres and white margins. It is a fairly strong grower, reaching 3m (10ft). '**Glacier**'☙, only 2m (6ft) high, has small,

Acacia baileyana 'Purpurea'

climber. A native of south-west Australia, it loves sun and well-drained soil; in cooler climates, it is best grown in a conservatory and will not do well out in the open air except in the most sheltered areas (see page 61). The nodding clusters of sky-blue, bell-shaped flowers are freely produced from summer to autumn. An evergreen twiner, it grows only 2m (6ft) high and will tuck into a small corner.

grey-green leaves mottled with silver-grey. It does not like cold winds. (See Good Companions, below.)

Jasminum nudiflorum☙ (see page 151) is well known for its golden flowers on bare stems in winter. '**Mystique**' has silver-variegated foliage that gives added interest in summer. It also makes the plant look lighter and more delicate. Happy in sun or shade, it grows to 3m (10ft).

GOOD COMPANIONS

The deep blue flowers of *Ceanothus* 'Puget Blue'☙ (1) make a fabulous contrast with the rich pink of the shrub rose *Rosa* NOBLE ANTONY ('Ausway') (2).

Pittosporum tenuifolium 'Irene Paterson'☙ (3) has creamy-white splashed leaves that make a perfect backdrop for the flowers of *Clematis* 'Kiri Te Kanawa' (4).

The soft silver of *Hedera helix* 'Glacier'☙ (5) works well with the purple flower spikes of the wallflower *Erysimum* 'Bowles' Mauve' (6), planted at its base.

Hedera helix 'Glacier'

Jasminum nudiflorum 'Mystique'

113

Coronilla valentina subsp. *glauca* 'Citrina' • *Cytisus battandieri* 'Yellow Tail' • *Schizophragma hydrangeoides* 'Moonlight' •

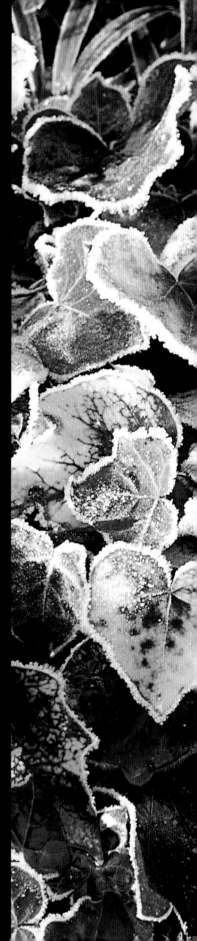

SEASONS

Spring is the season when climbers and wall shrubs begin to shine: plentiful blossom against a foil of fresh new foliage. Summer arrives with even more flamboyant flowers and richer fragrances. The cool autumn days change the palette as vibrant orange and fiery scarlet spread through leaves and polish berries. Winter, with its frost and low sun, highlights evergreen foliage but still produces some delicate blooms. Although most abundant in spring and summer, climbers play an important role on the garden stage throughout the year.

RIGHT: *Hedera helix* 'Angularis Aurea'.

Spring

Spring is a joyful season, a time of anticipation and renewal, when gardens start afresh with a clean slate. Spring-flowering climbers provide important visual balance to bulbs at ground level. Foliage and structure take a supporting role: flowers are the dominant feature of the season, often appearing on bare branches.

Afternoon sun catches the bronze young foliage and delicate pink flowers of *Clematis montana* var. *rubens* 'Pink Perfection'. The blooms have a fragrance reminiscent of vanilla.

Actinidia kolomikta

Actinidia pilosula

Although ***Actinidia kolomikta***♀ flowers in early summer with small, white or pink, fragrant flowers, its main season of interest is late spring, when the leaves look as if they have been dipped in white or pink paint. This bold variegation develops best in a sunny spot. The plant eventually reaches 4.5m (15ft) in height, and its twining stems need support, especially as cats seem to delight in rubbing against them. Any pruning needed to keep it within bounds should be done in early winter.

Actinidia pilosula is more delicate and not as tall, growing only to 3m (10ft). It has narrower, slightly smaller leaves, with white tips. The pink flowers appear earlier, in late spring, mingling attractively with the variegated leaves. Both these actinidias are extremely valuable for the length of time the leaves hold their colour, before it fades later in the season.

The blue of the spring-flowering cultivars of **ceanothus** (see page 111) perfectly suits the mood of the season, and fits in easily with spring bulbs in shades of blue and yellow. Evergreen wall shrubs, these ceanothus are fast-growing and easy to look after, and are ideal for quick effect. Be sure to check the flowering time when buying ceanothus, since some varieties bear their flowers later in the year, from late summer to autumn.

Camellia

Camellias are one of the few deep inky-green evergreens we have. Most species bloom in early spring, with their cultivars following in mid- to late spring. Flowers can be single, semi-double, double or formal double. Despite their exotic appearance, camellias are fairly hardy. With their compact, bushy habit, evergreen foliage and beautiful flowers, they look superb grown as wall shrubs and are excellent in pots (see pages 79–80).

Camellias are Asian plants by origin. Introduced to Britain in the 18th century, they were long considered too tender to survive outside. The Victorians especially loved their prim stiffness and they became treasured greenhouse plants. By the end of the 1920s gardeners had discovered that camellias could be grown outside and a breeding boom followed.

Woodland plants by nature, camellias love dappled shade and so thrive on shady walls, where the flowers are also protected from the damaging heat of early morning sunlight on frosty mornings (see page 42). They need an acid or neutral, humus-rich soil, which must be well drained. They are more lime-tolerant than rhododendrons, but in gardens where soil is limy they are best grown in containers. Use a soil-based ericaceous compost, which maintains its structure over a long time,

keeping it free-draining. A mulch with hardwood chips or slate scree helps to keep the roots cool.

Camellias need little attention once planted. They can be tied into trellis or wire, but do not need training. Pruning is necessary only if the plant outgrows its space and should be done as the main flush of flowers begins to fade. Camellias do need consistent watering, especially in summer, otherwise the developing flower buds will drop. Use a slow-release, ericaceous fertilizer annually at the correct dose – take care not to overfeed.

Camellia japonica is the main species but has been surpassed in popularity by the hybrid *Camellia × williamsii*, which flowers more freely and drops its fading blooms as they turn brown. *Camellia reticulata* (see page 59) and *Camellia sasanqua* (see page 149) are also worth growing, although both may need protection in cold climates.

Camellia 'Inspiration'♀ (1) produces pretty, semi-double, pink flowers from midwinter through to late spring. It reaches a height of 4m (13ft).

Camellia japonica 'Adolphe Audusson'♀ (2) is the classic double red camellia. Hardy and reliable, it flowers from mid- to late spring and grows to 5m (16ft).

Camellia japonica 'Alba Simplex' (3) is the most effective of the whites. It has single flowers, each with an attractive boss of golden stamens. It flowers from mid- to late spring and grows to 9m (30ft).

Camellia × williamsii 'Bow Bells'♀ (4) has single, rose-pink blooms, borne over a long season from late winter to late spring. The plant grows 4m (13ft) high.

Camellia × williamsii 'Debbie'♀ bears pink, peony-form flowers from mid- to late spring. It is upright and compact, growing to 5m (16ft), and useful in a narrow space.

Camellia × williamsii 'J.C. Williams'♀ produces beautiful single, soft shell-pink

flowers from early to mid-spring on a wide-spreading plant 5m (16ft) tall.

Camellia × williamsii 'Ruby Wedding'♀ has vivid red, peony-form flowers from mid- to late spring, and grows up to 5m (16ft) tall. The young growth is an attractive, rich red shade.

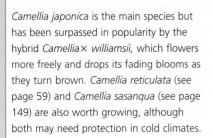

Chaenomeles

Chaenomeles are also known as ornamental or flowering quince, and are closely related to the common quince (*Cydonia*). In spring and summer they have simple, saucer-shaped flowers in shades of white, pink, red and apricot, with golden stamens; these are followed by aromatic fruit in late summer and autumn. The fruit is edible when cooked and can be used for making a jelly that is traditionally eaten with meat. With their stiffly branching habit, chaenomeles look awkward grown as free-standing shrubs. For this reason they are usually trained against a wall, where the flowers and fruit can more easily be enjoyed (see page 15). The ovate, green leaves appear during or after flowering.

There are two main species: *Chaenomeles japonica* and *Chaenomeles speciosa*. *Chaenomeles japonica* is low and spreading, and is ideal for training on walls up to 2m (6ft) high. It has orange, scarlet or blood-red flowers, borne after the foliage has broken in spring, and yellow fruit, sometimes flushed red.

Chaenomeles speciosa flowers earlier, usually starting in early spring before the foliage breaks. If the weather is not too harsh, it can sometimes be in flower even in early winter; it may also send out some late flowers in autumn. It grows larger than *Chaenomeles japonica*, reaching 4m (13ft) against a wall, and has larger, usually red flowers, followed by greenish-yellow fruit.

Chaenomeles speciosa 'Geisha Girl'♕ produces clusters of double flowers in a lovely shade of deep apricot-peach.

Chaenomeles × *superba* is a very popular cross between the two. It has flowers from early spring to midsummer, with cultivars in all shades from white through pink and red to orange, and has green fruit that ripen yellow. Against a wall it will reach 3m (10ft).

Chaenomeles are easy to grow with no special needs. They will be perfectly happy on a shady wall, although they flower and fruit best in sun. Training simply consists of tying in new growth. Pruning is confined to removing vigorous, outward-facing shoots that would otherwise hide the main framework carrying the flowers and fruit, and cutting back if the plant outgrows its allotted space. Any pruning should be done immediately after flowering.

Chaenomeles 'Madame Butterfly' has single, salmon-pink flowers splashed white.

Chaenomeles speciosa 'Yukigoten' (**1**) has the most exquisite semi-double, white flowers flushed with pale jade.

Chaenomeles superba 'Crimson and Gold'♕ (**2**) is an old hybrid that has really stood the test of time. The flowers are an intense shade of red with contrasting anthers.

Chaenomeles superba 'Jet Trail' produces masses of single, white flowers, even when young.

Chaenomeles superba 'Knap Hill Scarlet'♕ is a good older hybrid, with bright orange-scarlet flowers.

Chaenomeles superba 'Pink Lady'♕ has single, clear rose-pink flowers that are a deeper shade in bud. It is one of the earliest to flower.

SEASONS

Clematis armandii

Clematis 'Apple Blossom'

Clematis armandii 'Snowdrift'

Clematis armandii 'Enham Star'

Clematis 'Early Sensation'

Clematis armandii has always been much sought after. It is hard to propagate and the difficulty of obtaining it may have led to a belief that it is a better plant than it really is. At its best it is stunning, with large, evergreen, leathery leaves and, in early to mid-spring, dense clusters of creamy-white flowers with the scent of honey and almonds.

More often it suffers from chlorosis, which causes its leaves to turn yellow; there is a tendency for whole branches to die back; and it is susceptible to frost damage. It needs a sunny wall and protection from frost and cold winds; and it dislikes being trained so it is essential to let it find its own way. Choose a named variety to ensure that you get a good flowering plant, and be prepared to give it plenty of space since it will grow to a height of 6m (20ft).

Clematis 'Apple Blossom'♥ has broad white sepals, shaded with pink, and bronze-green leaves when young. The true variety is hard to find: because it is so difficult to propagate, inferior seedlings are often sold under this name. The same applies to *Clematis armandii* 'Snowdrift': the true variety has large,

fully rounded, clear white flowers, but is rarely seen. *Clematis armandii* 'Enham Star' is a recent hybrid with starry, white, scented flowers, very freely produced.

One of the most spectacular spring-flowering clematis is *Clematis* 'Early Sensation'. It is an evergreen hybrid, growing to 4m (13ft), one of a group raised in New Zealand using *Clematis paniculata*. It is not completely hardy and needs a sheltered position in well-drained soil; in cold areas it is safest to grow it in a conservatory. The foliage is leathery and finely cut and the flowers are simple and buttercup-like – this is one of the few clematis that advertises its membership of the buttercup family Ranunculaceae.

The flowers are a lovely creamy green when first open, changing to white as they age, and they usually completely smother the plant from mid- to late spring. This clematis has a second season of interest in autumn, when the mass of flowers is replaced by glorious fluffy, silvery seedheads.

The earliest of the large-flowered clematis hybrids flower from early spring to early summer, usually with a few more flowers in early autumn. They

CLEMATIS ALPINA

Clematis alpina♀ is a hardy, adaptable plant. It has nodding flowers in shades of blue, pink and white, with hanging sepals around an inner 'skirt' of petal-like stamens, making the flowers appear semi- or even fully double.

It responds rapidly to the onset of good weather so, although its main flowering season starts in mid-spring, in very mild areas some blooms may appear in midwinter. It is extremely free-flowering and a compact grower, with most varieties reaching around 2–3m (6–10ft) and needing very little pruning.

The foliage of the alpinas is a good, fresh, light green and covers well. If you leave the flowers on the plant, it will produce silky seedheads that last long after the leaves have fallen. This long season of interest makes it an ideal choice for growing on a garden feature. It is an excellent companion for other plants and will happily grow through many larger shrubs and small trees. It is also extremely hardy, one of the few clematis that thrive in cold climates.

Unlike most other clematis, the alpinas have very fine roots. These are susceptible to damage through waterlogging so never plant them deeply (see page 29). Alpinas also grow best in poorer soils. With these requirements satisfied, they will then thrive in sun or shade.

Clematis **'Frances Rivis'**♀ (**1**) is the best-known variety. It is the deepest blue, has the longest, most elegant flowers and is very free-flowering. In mainland Europe a different form is sold, which has much shorter, blunter sepals.

Clematis **'Ocean Pearl'** (**2**) is a new introduction with fully double flowers, unique in the alpina-type hybrids, produced at the same time as the normal singles. The sepals are violet-blue, with the single flowers showing a white 'skirt' beneath.

Clematis **'Constance'**♀ (**3**) is a fabulous deep pink with short, blunt sepals that open out wide. The outer petal-like stamens are also pink and almost as long as the sepals, making the flowers appear semi-double.

Clematis **'Frankie'**♀ (**4**) has mauve-blue sepals with a white 'skirt'. It produces a good crop of late flowers.

Clematis **'Jacqueline du Pré'**♀ (**5**) produces deep pink bells with a light pink margin.

OTHER GOOD CLEMATIS ALPINA

Clematis **'Burford White'** White with blunt sepals, giving the flowers a more rounded appearance. Stands up to bad weather better than many other white-flowered climbers. (See Good Companions, opposite.)

Clematis **'Columbine'** Clear, light to mid-blue flowers fading to powder blue.

Clematis **'Willy'** Very pale mauve-pink blooms with a shot of deep rose at the base of the sepals.

Clematis JOSEPHINE

Clematis 'Mrs Cholmondeley'

Clematis 'Vyvyan Pennell'

grow to 2.5–3m (8–10ft). Unfortunately, although they are some of the most beautiful hybrids, they are also the most susceptible to clematis wilt (see page 63), having *Clematis lanuginosa*, the species believed to carry the genetic weakness, in their breeding. Good hybrids include **Clematis 'Elsa Späth'**, which has 18cm (7in), lavender-blue flowers with red anthers; **'H.F. Young'**, freely producing 20cm (8in) blue flowers with yellow anthers (see page 78); and JOSEPHINE ('Evijohill')♔, which has double, pale pink flowers with a deeper stripe. **'Mrs Cholmondeley'**♔ (pronounced chumley) has pale lavender-blue flowers, with widely spaced sepals and toffee-coloured anthers. **'Vyvyan Pennell'** has lovely, rich purple-blue, double flowers, but it is the most susceptible to clematis wilt.

Forsythia suspensa (see pages 88–89) is a classic, deciduous, spring-flowering wall shrub, not as well known as its more shrubby relations. It has elegant, lax stems, which create a waterfall of shimmering golden bells 4m (13ft) high.

For early fragrance *Holboellia coriacea* (China blue vine) is unbeatable: the small, hanging, bell-like, white flowers, some with a purple flush, have a very rich scent, stronger than honeysuckle. The evergreen foliage is akin to that of *Akebia* and *Stauntonia* (see pages 41 and 50), to which it is related. It will need shelter from cold wind, but in a very hot summer will produce mauve, sausage-shaped fruit. Growing quite large, to 7m (22ft), it is not really suitable for small gardens.

GOOD COMPANIONS

The silver foliage of *Lavandula* × *chaytorae* 'Sawyers'♔ (1) looks lovely at the base of alpina-type *Clematis* 'Burford White' (2), contrasting with its fresh green foliage and its white flowers.

The white papery blooms of *Cistus* × *obtusifolius* 'Thrive' (3) open after the elegant, alpina-type *Clematis* 'Helsingborg'♔ (4) has finished flowering. Both plants love the same soil conditions.

A pair for interest over three seasons: *Pyracantha* 'Golden Charmer'♔ (5) blooms after alpina-type *Clematis* 'Blue Dancer' (6); in autumn, the clematis seedheads sit beautifully with the pyracantha berries.

Holboellia coriacea

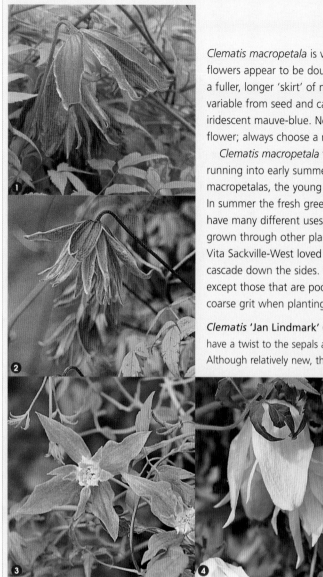

CLEMATIS MACROPETALA

Clematis macropetala is very similar to *Clematis alpina* (see page 120). Its nodding flowers appear to be double, consisting of an outer group of sepals surrounding a fuller, longer 'skirt' of narrower, pointed, petal-like stamens. The species is very variable from seed and can be anything from a weak powder blue to a stunning iridescent mauve-blue. Never buy an unnamed species clone unless you see it in flower; always choose a named variety.

   Clematis macropetala flowers after *Clematis alpina*, starting in late spring and running into early summer. It is deciduous and grows to 2.5m (8ft). With all the macropetalas, the young shoots and flowers are covered with delicate downy hairs. In summer the fresh green, divided foliage has a charm of its own. The macropetalas have many different uses, being good in sun or shade and either on their own or grown through other plants. They are also fabulous for containers (see page 80); Vita Sackville-West loved to plant them in big Ali Baba pots and allow them to cascade down the sides. Free-flowering and easy to grow, macropetalas like all soils except those that are poorly drained in winter. If your soil is heavy, add plenty of coarse grit when planting.

Clematis **'Jan Lindmark'** (**1**) has the earliest flowers. These are a beautiful mauve and have a twist to the sepals and petal-like stamens that makes them look especially full. Although relatively new, this variety is deservedly popular.

Clematis macropetala **'Lagoon'**♀ (see Good Companions, below) is the largest and darkest of the blues. To get the best effect from the flowers, plant it against a light background.

Clematis macropetala **'Wesselton'** (**2**) is similar to the species. The flowers are the same good mauve-blue, but they are larger.

Clematis **'Markham's Pink'**♀ (see Good Companions, below) has proven star quality, having been a favourite since its introduction in 1935. The flowers are sugar pink with a fine pale margin. In full sun the colour is clear pink, while in shade more mauve shows through.

Clematis **'Pauline'** (**3**) has very large, blue flowers. Strong-growing and free-flowering, it is one of the best of its kind.

Clematis **'Purple Spider'** has fabulous deep purple-blue flowers, but the plant is weak-growing.

Clematis **'White Wings'** (**4**) is the best of the white macropetalas, with well-shaped, creamy-white flowers.

GOOD COMPANIONS

Sometimes keeping plant combinations really simple – such as using two varieties of the same species in contrasting colours – brings outstanding results. The sugar-pink *Clematis* 'Markham's Pink'♀ (1) looks stunning with the deep blue *Clematis macropetala* 'Lagoon'♀ (2).

CLEMATIS MONTANA

Clematis montana is a vigorous, deciduous climber with masses of small flowers in late spring and early summer. The flowers of the species itself are single and white, but in many cultivated forms they are double and pink. With most varieties reaching 8m (26ft), this clematis is excellent for covering larger areas and growing into trees (see page 68). It is also happy in shade, although the pink varieties do lose colour.

The divided foliage is green in the white-flowered forms and variably flushed with bronze in the pink varieties. Despite appearances, *Clematis montana* is not the hardiest of clematis: a late spring frost can destroy the flower buds and sometimes even cause damage to the plant itself.

Clematis 'Broughton Star'♧ is very pretty, with double, dusky pink flowers with darker markings. It is compact, reaching just 5m (16ft), and makes an excellent partner for smaller trees. It needs a sunny spot and may not be the toughest of varieties.

Clematis 'Christine' (**1**) is a new cultivar, growing to 6m (20ft), with large, clear white flowers with a pink reverse, giving the impression of apple blossom. The pink is a clean shade without the hint of yellow that is in many of the montana varieties.

Clematis 'Freda'♧ (**2**) is a deep cherry red with a slightly paler centre to each sepal. It is a good, compact form, reaching 6m (20ft), with bronze young foliage (see also page 44). If space is more limited choose *Clematis* 'Picton's Variety', which grows to 4.5m (15ft). A pretty mauve-pink, it tends to send out the occasional midsummer flower.

Clematis 'Gothenburg' is an uncommon variety from Sweden. It has bronze leaves with a slightly lighter central strip, similar to a mild variegation, and creamy-pink flowers on a compact plant that will grow to 5m (16ft).

Clematis montana var. *grandiflora*♧ (**3**) has larger flowers than the species but is smaller-growing, reaching just 5m (16ft). It is good for a shady wall, the white blooms standing out from the darkness.

Clematis montana var. *rubens* 'Tetrarose'♧ (**4**) has large, dark rosy-mauve flowers with a satiny sheen. The foliage is bronze, maturing to deep purple. It grows up to 7.5m (25ft) and is probably the best of the pink montanas

OTHER GOOD CLEMATIS MONTANA

Clematis montana var. *rubens* 'Pink Perfection' Has vanilla-scented, pink flowers and bronze foliage. Vigorous, reaching 8–10m (26–33ft). (See pages 68 and 116.)

Clematis montana var. *wilsonii* Blooms later than the species, in mid- to late summer, producing large, white, chocolate-scented flowers with a slightly undulating margin. Grows to 10m (33ft).

Clematis 'Primrose Star' (**5**) is a fairly new form with semi-double flowers in an attractive shade of creamy primrose, fading quickly to white in sun. Sometimes they show flecks of pink. Reaching an easy 7m (22ft), the plant is not as bushy as some montanas and so makes a good choice for a pergola. The flowers are not as abundant as in other varieties.

Clematis 'Sunrise' (**6**) is another new introduction, a very free-flowering plant with excellent double, rich, dark pink flowers massed over dark bronze foliage. It is a clearer pink than 'Broughton Star' and seems to be hardier. It grows to 7m (22ft).

Wisteria

Wisteria is without doubt the king of climbers. A vigorous, twining, deciduous climber, growing to 9m (30ft), it has bold, pinnate foliage that often colours well in autumn. The flowers are mostly in shades of blue to violet, but there are also white or pink forms; they are usually scented and are borne in long, hanging racemes most often just before the leaves appear. Wisterias often produce long, velvety seedpods but these may contain only one seed.

Fossil evidence shows that wisterias have been around for at least seven million years and possibly much, much longer. They are native to China, Japan and the eastern USA, where they grow freely in moist woodland and on stream banks. The American species *Wisteria frutescens* was introduced to Europe in 1724; the Japanese wisteria, *Wisteria floribunda*, and the Chinese *Wisteria sinensis*♀ (see page 10) were both brought back to Europe in the early 1800s.

In Europe, forms of the Chinese and Japanese wisterias are those most commonly cultivated. Traditionally these two species have been distinguished by the direction in which they twine: the Japanese clockwise and the Chinese anti-clockwise. As the species have been crossed, however, this distinction is becoming blurred. In the past the raceme length has also been a key to identification, with *floribunda* having much longer flowerheads than *sinensis*, but that distinction too is fading.

Wisterias need a sunny position in relatively good soil. Do not overfeed them or they will produce too

Long, elegant flower racemes typify the Japanese wisteria, *Wisteria floribunda*. Pruning twice a year will encourage the best display.

much leaf and no flowers. A good plant will be grafted onto a rootstock, in order to give flowers at the earliest possible stage. Seedling wisterias are almost always inferior, and will not produce flowers for many years. Even with grafted stock you may have to wait five years for flowers to appear.

For the Japanese, wisteria culture is an art form and ancient plants often have their own temple alongside. Huge bamboo structures are also constructed to allow plants to spread to their ultimate height. Visitors pay to see these plants, having tea under the blossoms, and tie messages onto the branches for good luck. In the West we are less flamboyant in our use of wisterias, confining them to house walls and pergolas or training them as standards. Pruning and training is straightforward (see page 34) but time-consuming and very physical, so never let wisteria grow beyond a manageable height.

***Wisteria brachybotrys* 'Shiro-kapitan'** has very fragrant, large, white flowers in short, blunt racemes, 15cm (6in) long. The plant may suffer frost damage and it may be a little shy to flower.

OTHER GOOD WISTERIAS

Wisteria 'Burford' Heavily scented, deep bluish-purple and lilac flowers in racemes 40cm (16in) long. (See page 83.)

Wisteria 'Caroline' Distinctive off-white and lavender flowers, faintly scented, in racemes 20cm (8in) long. Early flowering.

Wisteria floribunda 'Royal Purple' Very elegant, strongly coloured, dark lavender flowers in racemes 40cm (16in) long. Only slightly scented. Has good autumn colour.

Wisteria sinensis 'Alba' ♡ Faintly scented, white flowers with a hint of lilac, in narrow racemes 25cm (10in) long. Lemon-yellow leaves in autumn.

WISTERIA FLOWERS

The wisteria flowerhead is like that of a lupin or sweet pea, but with one important difference: the raceme hangs down. The flowers have evolved to be pollinated by bees: it takes the weight of a bee landing on the keel petal to push it down and expose the stamens within. To enable pollination to occur, the flower has to rotate through 180° between the time when the raceme develops and the time when the individual flower opens to allow the bee to land on the keel.

Wisteria sinensis 'Amethyst' (1) is a vigorous variety with deep bronze young foliage. The racemes, 18cm (7in) long, are a much deeper shade of violet-blue than normal and are exceptionally scented. Although the autumn colour is not strong, this is one of the best *sinensis* varieties.

Wisteria floribunda 'Alba' ♡ (2) is a beautiful white form with elegant racemes, 45cm (18in) long, and light apple-green foliage. It flowers late, in early summer. Monet chose this variety for the Japanese bridge in his garden at Giverny, France. (See also page 92.)

Wisteria floribunda 'Multijuga' ♡ (formerly known as 'Macrobotrys') has the most glorious lavender racemes, which can be 1m (40in) long or more. This is not because each raceme has more flowers than other cultivars, but because the flowers are more widely spaced.

Wisteria floribunda 'Violacea Plena' (3) takes time to bloom, but when it does it produces beautiful, double, violet-blue flowers in racemes 35cm (14in) long. It has the best autumn leaf colour.

Wisteria frutescens (American wisteria) has slightly ruffled, purple flowers, produced on racemes 30–60cm (12–24in) long in summer. The flowers are extremely pretty but because they appear later, mixed in among the leaves, the display is less showy than in other wisterias.

Early summer

Early summer brings the first flush of abundant flower. Gardens are alive with colour, foliage is lush and green, and gorgeous scent fills the air. Most of our favourite climbers perform at this time, with jasmines, clematis, honeysuckles and roses all vying for attention.

Rosa 'Madame Grégoire Staechelin' has flowers in abundance in summer and a glorious scent.

The divas of the **clematis** world, the large-flowered doubles, show their colours in early summer. They are bold and exciting and grow to just 2.5–3m (8–10ft), making them ideal for smaller gardens. Generally they have double flowers on the growth produced the previous year, followed by singles on the later growth.

Clematis ARCTIC QUEEN ('Evitwo')♀ is a new hybrid that has double flowers on both old and new growth. The flowers, approximately 18cm (7in) across, are white with creamy-yellow anthers and are produced in good quantities.

Clematis 'Proteus' is an especially beautiful double with lavender-pink flowers. It will thrive best in a semi-shaded position, perhaps with late afternoon sun. Once established it is a good grower. The single flowers in late summer are extremely pretty and it looks lovely with *Lavandula* 'Regal Splendour' at its base.

(continued on page 133)

Clematis ARCTIC QUEEN

Clematis 'Proteus'

OTHER GOOD DOUBLE CLEMATIS

Clematis **'Countess of Lovelace'** Bluish-lilac flowers with extremely pointed sepals.

Clematis **'Fairy Blue'** (CRYSTAL FOUNTAIN) Elegant, light blue flowers that are often suffused with violet.

Clematis **'Kathleen Dunford'** Semi-double, purplish-pink flowers with narrow sepals.

Clematis **'Walter Pennell'** Grey-purple flowers with cream anthers.

Jasmine (Jasminum)

The summer-flowering jasmine or jessamine was first written about in 1415, but is believed to have been grown for much longer. It is known that there were double-flowered and silver-leaved forms of summer jasmine, which have slipped out of cultivation, plus a golden form, which has only recently reappeared. Jasmine's fall in popularity was probably caused by the demise of great houses with their showy conservatories and orangeries. Today, there are only a few species that we can grow easily outdoors in cooler climates. (See also pages 102–103. For shrubby, winter-flowering jasmines see pages 99 and 113.)

Summer jasmines are mostly quick-growing, twining climbers with richly scented, starry, white flowers and deep green, pinnate leaves. They love a hot, sunny position with sandy, well-drained soil. Feed sparingly since plants that are too well fed and leafy produce less fragrant flowers. Pruning should be undertaken as the first flush of flowers fades.

Jasminum officinale♚, the common or poet's jasmine, has long been a popular inhabitant of cottage gardens and is used commercially in the production of essential oils. It grows to 12m (40ft), is semi-evergreen and produces deliciously scented flowers from early summer to early autumn. It needs a sheltered position in colder regions.

OTHER GOOD JASMINES

Jasminum beesianum Tiny, deep velvety pink, slightly fragrant flowers, in late spring and early summer, among evergreen foliage, and followed by glossy black berries. Height 3.5m (12ft).

Jasminum × *stephanense* Fragrant pink flowers in early to midsummer. Young leaves often variegated with cream. Height 7.5m (25ft).

Jasminum officinale 'Clotted Cream' (1) is a recent introduction, with wonderfully fragrant, prominently held flowers of a lovely creamy-parchment colour.

Jasminum officinale 'Argenteovariegatum'♚ (2) has grey-green leaves, margined creamy white and sometimes flushed with pink. (See Good Companions, page 133.)

Jasminum officinale 'Inverleith'♚ (3) is striking – bright red in bud, with the

red colour remaining on the back of the lobes when the flower opens. The colour is especially good on young growth and in cool conditions.

Jasminum officinale f. *affine* is a superior form of the common jasmine that used to be known as *Jasminum officinale* 'Grandiflorum'. The slightly larger flowers and buds, tinged pink on the outside, mean that it is the most often-seen representative of the species.

Honeysuckle (Lonicera)

The genus *Lonicera* is a very varied one, including deciduous and evergreen, shrubby and climbing species. Even the climbing varieties vary between scandent shrubs, sending up long shoots that find their way through the branches of other shrubs, and true twining climbers. Climbing honeysuckles grow to anything from 4m (13ft) to 10m (33ft) and the foliage is generally oval and matt green.

The often richly perfumed flowers, borne mainly in summer, are funnel- or trumpet-shaped, usually in terminal clusters but sometimes produced along the stems; they are pollinated by hawkmoths or bumble bees, attracted in many cases by the strong scent. Flower colour ranges from soft cream through yellow and orange, often flushed with red or pink. (See also pages 49, 52–53, 73, 82, 107 and 137.)

Being a woodland plant, honeysuckle needs a cool root run, in humus-rich soil. If it gets too hot and dry it is extremely susceptible to mildew and aphid attack. If it is deprived of water it loses foliage and the stems become very twisted and stunted. It does sometimes die back, but this is a natural occurrence and the dead growth should simply be cut away; the plant will grow again quite happily. Pruning is needed only when the plant has outgrown the allotted space and should be done immediately after flowering.

The common honeysuckle or woodbine is one of the loveliest plants of the British countryside. Both *Lonicera caprifolium*♥ and *Lonicera periclymenum* inhabit the hedgerows and woods, their heady scent making a walk down a country lane a delight. Honeysuckle was cultivated in gardens in London as far back as 1286, and has always been very much part of gardening history (see pages 9–10).

Lonicera periclymenum 'Belgica' (left) is the wonderfully fragrant early Dutch honeysuckle, freely producing rich creamy-yellow flowers flushed with pink from early to midsummer. It is deciduous and grows to 7m (22ft).

Lonicera × *tellmanniana* (below) has real zing. The flowers, borne in early and midsummer, are rich coppery orange, but unfortunately unscented. It prefers semi- or complete shade and loamy soil. It is deciduous, growing to 5m (16ft).

Lonicera periclymenum 'Graham Thomas'♀ (**1**) grows to 7m (22ft) and has richly scented, creamy-yellow flowers all summer.

Lonicera caprifolium♀ (**2**) is probably the earliest to flower of the summer

honeysuckles. It is often confused with *Lonicera periclymenum* (see page 82), but is easily distinguished as the two leaves under each flower are fused together, making one round or oval leaf that encircles the stem. Richly scented, white and creamy-yellow flowers with a pink flush are borne all summer. It is deciduous and grows to 6m (20ft).

Lonicera similis var. *delavayi*♀ (**3**) is the civilized cousin of *Lonicera japonica* (see pages 52–53): it has semi-evergreen, more elegant, larger foliage and equally scented flowers without the rampant habit, reaching just 5m (16ft). The flowers, borne from summer to autumn, are creamy white then yellow.

Lonicera periclymenum 'Serotina'♀ (**4**), the late Dutch or late red honeysuckle, has blue-green foliage flushed with red on the young growths. The richly scented, creamy-yellow flowers are also heavily flushed dark pink. It grows to 7m (22ft) and blooms from midsummer into autumn.

Lonicera periclymenum 'Munster' (**5**) has scented, broad-petalled pink flowers from early to late summer. It reaches 7m (22ft).

Lonicera periclymenum 'Sweet Sue' (**6**) is strongly scented, with creamy-yellow flowers from early to late summer. It is relatively compact, to 5m (16ft). (See Good Companions, page 133.)

OTHER GOOD HONEYSUCKLES

Lonicera × *italica*♀ (also incorrectly known as *Lonicera* × *americana*) Deciduous climber, 7m (22ft) tall, with very fragrant, pink-flushed yellow flowers borne all summer, followed by red berries.

Lonicera × *italica* HARLEQUIN ('Sherlite') Has bright green leaves edged with cream and pink. Height 7m (22ft).

Lonicera japonica var. *repens*♀ Has red-flushed growth, and cream flowers ageing to yellow from early summer to mid-autumn. Good for ground cover. Grows to 10m (33ft).

Lonicera 'Mandarin' Dramatic but scentless, large, pink and yellow-orange flowers from early to midsummer. Height 6m (20ft).

Lonicera tragophylla♀ Very large, unscented, bright golden yellow flowers in early and midsummer. Extremely showy. Needs complete shade. Height 6m (20ft).

129

CLIMBING AND RAMBLING ROSES

Climbing and rambling roses are very special garden plants: there is nothing quite like the beauty of their flowers or the delightful fragrance with which they fill our gardens. They have gained a reputation for being slightly difficult to grow, but given rich soil and plentiful food, they will reward with an unmatched season of flower.
(See also pages 57, 64–65, 70, 84–85, 94–95, 100 and 108–109.)

CLIMBING ROSES

Some roses are true climbers, but many are strong-growing sports (randomly occurring variants) of bush roses. The prefix 'climbing' in front of the name indicates this. All build up a framework of branches from which the flowering wood grows. Pruning consists of a light trim annually and the occasional removal of one of the oldest shoots to encourage the plant to produce strong new growth (see page 30). Training stems as near to horizontal as possible encourages more flower buds to form.

Climbing roses have a stiff habit and look better when accompanied by another climber such as a sweet pea (*Lathyrus odoratus*) or passion flower (*Passiflora*). Their strong stems mean that they are excellent for training on fences and walls and, because they build up a permanent framework, they make better cover than ramblers for unsightly objects. Some climbing roses bloom only once in summer, but many flower repeatedly all through the season.

Rosa 'Climbing Lady Hillingdon'♀ is a real gem. The flowers open from elegant, pointed buds to large, loose blooms with a fabulous tea rose scent; they are the most glorious shade of rich apricot with a hint of yellow. Growing to 5m (16ft), with masses of luxuriant, glossy foliage, it is the best of the climbing tea roses and is surprisingly hardy. It will perform best when grown against a warm wall, where it will flower repeatedly throughout the summer.

Also known as the old glory rose, *Rosa* 'Gloire de Dijon' (1) has huge charm and is a cottage-garden favourite. It grows to 5m (16ft) and has large, flat, almost crumpled-looking, buff-yellow flowers opening from rounded buds. It is richly scented. One of the first climbers in flower, it produces a main crop in early summer, and a few more throughout the rest of the season. It needs feeding well, both in spring and midsummer.

The noisette rose *Rosa* 'Madame Alfred Carrière'♀ (2) flowers freely all through summer and produces large, sweetly scented, translucent white blooms flushed with flesh pink in the centre. Vigorous and extremely healthy, it has very upright growth, reaching 7m (22ft).

Rosa 'Madame Grégoire Staechelin'♀ (3) is also known as 'Spanish Beauty'. Although it has only one flush of flowers, in early summer, it is so beautiful that it is worth giving it the 7m (22ft) of space it needs. Your reward will be billowing masses of clear, vibrant pink flowers, as much as 12.5cm (5in) across and with the scent of sweet peas, hanging in clusters along the branches. (See also page 126.)

Rosa 'New Dawn'♀ (4) was introduced in 1930 but is still one of the most popular roses sold. Blush-pink flowers with a silvery sheen and a fresh, fruity fragrance are borne on a plant 3.5m (12ft) tall. It blooms freely throughout the summer. It also drops the fading flowers, giving a clean, fresh appearance to the plant as the season progresses. (See Good Companions, page 133.)

RAMBLING ROSES

Ramblers shoot from the base, often producing really long stems that need tying into their support. Gardening books used to recommend removing all the old flowering stems every year, but this is unnecessary. Simply remove one third of the oldest flowering shoots each year after flowering. This will be enough to stop the base becoming overcrowded. If, however, you are growing a rambler in a less formal situation, up a tree for example, pruning may not be necessary, or even desirable, as it can result in stems being dislodged from the tree.

Ramblers have different characteristics depending on their breeding: some are stiff in habit, ideal for growing through trees; others are slender and graceful, and are more suited to pergolas and arches. Most have only a single flush of flowers, in early and midsummer.

OTHER GOOD CLIMBING AND RAMBLING ROSES

Rosa 'Alister Stella Gray' Climber with neatly scrolled, rich egg-yellow buds opening to fully double, rosette-shaped flowers, with a tea rose scent. Flowers from early summer to early autumn. Height 5m (16ft).

Rosa 'Desprez à Fleurs Jaunes' Climber with richly scented flowers in warm yellow, shaded with peach and apricot, from early summer to early autumn. Height 6m (20ft).

Rosa 'Emily Gray' Rambler with semi-double, buff-yellow, scented flowers in summer. Height 4m (13ft).

Rosa 'Francis E. Lester'♥ Rambler producing single, white flowers with pink edges in midsummer. Richly scented. Small orange hips in autumn. Height 4.5m (15ft).

Rosa 'Leverkusen'♥ Lemon-scented climber with rosette-shaped, pale yellow flowers in early and midsummer, with a few blooms in late summer. Height 3.5m (12ft).

Rosa 'Pink Perpétué' Bright pink climber. Flowers in early and mid-summer with a few blooms in late summer. Slightly fragrant. Height 5m (16ft).

Rosa 'Félicité Perpétué'♥ (1) is a fantastic rose producing large clusters of creamy-white, pompon flowers, with a primrose fragrance, in midsummer. The buds are dark pink, making a charming contrast with the open flowers. It has strong, healthy foliage and grows to 7m (22ft). Introduced in 1827, it is still one of the very best ramblers.

Rosa 'François Juranville'♥ (2) has coral-pink, double flowers, opening flat on graceful, arching growth, mainly in early summer, with some blooms later in the season. It grows to 6m (20ft) and has a sharp apple fragrance.

Rosa 'Albertine'♥ (3) is a strongly scented rambler, with large, coppery-pink flowers in early and midsummer. It grows to 7m (22ft).

Rosa 'Veilchenblau'♥ (4), a distinctive rambler, has dark magenta flowers that fade to lilac, appearing almost blue as they age. They have a strong orange scent and are borne in midsummer. It grows to 5m (16ft) and has virtually thornless stems.

Rosa 'Paul's Himalayan Musk'♥ is a pink rambler with dainty, hanging sprays on long, trailing stems and with a strong, musky fragrance. It flowers in profusion in early and midsummer and is big and bold enough to make a really effective feature. It needs space, growing to 10m (33ft). (See page 70.)

MINIATURE CLIMBING ROSES

Only introduced in the 1990s, miniature climbing roses are not simply small-growing climbers but are scaled down in all their parts. They are ideally suited to today's smaller gardens, where space is limited, and this group of climbers is likely to expand greatly in time. They grow to 2.5m (8ft) and have a stiffly upright habit. The scented flowers are carried from top to bottom of the plant and so these roses are an ideal choice for pillars and posts. They are very easy to care for, needing only minimal pruning if they outgrow the space allotted to them. Regular deadheading will ensure that they flower from early summer to early autumn.

Rosa GLORIANA ('Chewpope') has double, grape-purple flowers with a light scent. It is slightly larger than the other cultivars, reaching 3m (10ft).

Rosa LAURA FORD ('Chewarvel')♛ (1) is one of the two original introductions and has proved extremely popular. It has neat, double, deep yellow flowers with a flush of orange and a strong fragrance.

Rosa NICE DAY ('Chewsea')♛ has pretty clusters of slightly scented, double, salmon-pink flowers carried above shiny, bronze to mid-green leaves.

Rosa SUMMERTIME ('Chewlarmoll') is the first miniature climber to win the Rose of the Year award. The soft creamy-yellow flowers have a deeper centre and are scented.

Rosa WARM WELCOME ('Chewizz')♛ (2), the second of the original introductions, has brilliant orange-red, fragrant flowers. Although the shape of the blooms is not perfect, it flowers extremely well.

OTHER GOOD MINIATURE CLIMBING ROSES

Rosa GOOD AS GOLD ('Chewsunbeam') Fragrant, pure golden yellow, double flowers.

Rosa LITTLE RAMBLER ('Chewramb')♛ Very fragrant, palest pink flowers. Height 2m (6ft).

Rosa LOVE KNOT ('Chewglorious') Scented, dark red blooms.

WHERE TO SEE ROSES

The Garden of Historic Roses (National Trust for Scotland) at Drum Castle, near Banchory, Aberdeenshire, is divided into four parts, the design of each quadrant and the roses planted in it being taken from the 17th, 18th, 19th or 20th century. This is a peaceful spot, heady with the perfume of old-fashioned shrub and climbing roses.

In the south of England, the walled rose gardens created by rose expert Graham Stuart Thomas at Mottisfont Abbey (National Trust), near Romsey, Hampshire, are a lesson in companion planting. Old roses (a National Collection), clematis and herbaceous perennials provide a quintessentially English garden mix of colour and scent.

ESTABLISHING CLIMBING AND RAMBLING ROSES

Remember that roses are greedy feeders and you will not go far wrong. They fare better on clay soils, which hold plenty of nutrients, than on light, sandy or chalky soils, which tend to be leached of nutrients and dry out quickly. Dig the soil well before planting; add a layer of well-rotted horse manure at the bottom of the hole, cover this with a layer of soil and then plant the rose. Choose a good-quality rose food and feed twice yearly, first in early spring, when the rose starts to grow, and again at the end of early summer, when the first flush of flower is fading.

Clematis 'Duchess of Edinburgh' (see page 78) is probably one of the best known of the large-flowered doubles, with white flowers on both old and new wood. The earlier flowers tend to have a green flush on the sepals, as do those of the stunning double *Clematis* 'Vyvyan Pennell' (see page 121).

Lathyrus odoratus (sweet pea) seems to capture the very essence of summer: filling the house with bunches fresh from the garden is a huge treat. (See Good Companions, below.) *Lathyrus odoratus* 'Cupani' is the original, richly scented, deep purple and pink sweet pea, from which most varieties are descended. These annual, tendril climbers bloom from summer to early autumn. Most varieties reach 2.5m (8ft) in height and the flowers come in a rainbow of colours excluding only orange and yellow. Grow sweet peas in a sunny spot, in moist but well-drained, fertile soil, and water regularly to avoid powdery mildew. Also,

Lathyrus odoratus

deadhead them frequently to promote flowering. Sweet peas are easily raised from seed, but choosing varieties is more difficult. If you are new to growing sweet peas then choose a seed mixture; most good seed companies offer a range based on characteristics such as height, colour or scent. For most gardeners, scent is the primary requirement. As your experience grows, experiment with named varieties.

Lathyrus latifolius 'Red Pearl'

Lathyrus latifolius 'White Pearl'

To start with, choose ones that you see sold as young plants in garden centres – it is a sign that they are worth growing.

Lathyrus latifolius ♥ (perennial pea) is an alternative, if you don't have time to raise plants from seed. It is a herbaceous perennial, growing to 3m (10ft), that forms a dense clump of shoots. For this reason it needs to be given space at the base, perhaps with a small shrub to help disguise the messy habit. Flowers are produced from early summer through to late autumn, but they lack the scent of their annual cousins. Forms include 'Rosa Perle' ♥, which has pale pink flowers, 'Red Pearl', which is dark pink, and 'White Pearl' ♥, which is pure white.

GOOD COMPANIONS

For a colourful pairing, underplant the creamy-variegated *Jasminum officinale* 'Argenteovariegatum' ♥ (1) with the velvety purple flowers of *Vinca minor* 'Atropurpurea' (2).

Lonicera periclymenum 'Sweet Sue' (3) looks gorgeous planted with the climbing rose *Rosa* 'New Dawn' ♥ (4). The soft colouring of both makes an unusual combination.

Richly scented sweet peas (*Lathyrus odoratus*) (5) are classic cottage-garden favourites and look wonderful combined with pink dahlias, such as *Dahlia* 'Art Nouveau' (6).

Late summer

Late summer brings with it a whole new flush of flower. Those plants with a bolder, more exotic feel come into the limelight now, boosted by the longer days and often baking heat. The colour palette changes from soft pastels to strong, rich colours, particularly vibrant in the many forms of texensis and viticella clematis.

Late summer is often a neglected season and gardens tend to tumble into an early decline towards autumn. Frequently, holidays are the main focus of attention, keeping us from visiting garden centres and nurseries and seeing what is flourishing there. Bedding plants dominate the season and we forget about perennial plants that do not have to be replaced year after year. Use perennial climbers and wall shrubs and they will perform for years and give the garden a much more exciting feel.

If you have planted late-summer climbers, earlier care in their cultivation will pay off now as plants with healthy, fresh-looking leaves show off their flowers much better than battle-worn

Late-flowering *Clematis* 'Prince Charles' scrambles engagingly through late blooms of *Rosa* 'Madame Alfred Carrière'.

specimens. A feed with a good all-round fertilizer is welcome at this stage, giving plants a boost.

Berberidopsis corallina, the coral plant, is an exotic oddity in that it loves a shady position but needs heat to thrive.

A native of Chile, it grows in the forests near Coronel. It is hard to please and demands a deep, moist soil with shelter from drying winds. It will tolerate some lime in the soil if peat or peat-free ericaceous compost is added, but will not grow on chalk. If you can provide the right conditions it is worth growing, otherwise it will prove disappointing. It is an evergreen, scrambling climber, growing to 5m (16ft). From summer to early autumn, red, bell-shaped flowers, resembling those of berberis, are arranged along the ends of the branches below the long, heart-shaped, green leaves.

Campsis (see page 39) add a rich tropical feel to the garden with their trumpet-shaped flowers in shades of yellow, orange, apricot and terracotta, borne in late summer and early autumn. The deciduous growth is self-clinging and varieties like **Campsis × tagliabuana 'Madame Galen'**♀ make wonderful hosts for late-flowering clematis. (See Good Companions, page 137.)

The late-flowering **ceanothus** also come into their own now. *Ceanothus* **'Autumnal Blue'**♀ and **'Burkwoodii'**♀ both provide the unusual combination of evergreen foliage and late flowers: the best of both worlds. 'Autumnal Blue' is by far the hardier, coping well with low temperatures. It has abundant panicles of sky-blue flowers from late summer to autumn and even sometimes gives a few bonus flowers in the spring. 'Burkwoodii' has rich, bright blue flowers with darker stamens from midsummer to mid-autumn, but it needs a more sheltered spot. Both will reach 3m (10ft) against a wall.

Ceanothus × delileanus 'Gloire de Versailles'♀, although deciduous, is more tender. It has large panicles of soft blue flowers from midsummer to mid-autumn. **Ceanothus × pallidus 'Perle**

Soft blue *Ceanothus × delileanus* 'Gloire de Versailles' blends with the scented flowers of *Hemerocallis lilioasphodelus*, the lemon lily.

Campsis × tagliabuana 'Madame Galen'

Ceanothus × pallidus 'Perle Rose'

Clematis 'Prince Charles'

Rose' produces bright rose-carmine flowers, which vary slightly in intensity in different soils. Growing to 3m (10ft), both love a hot, sunny site in reasonably good soil and are best protected from cold winds.

There is a group of large-flowered **clematis** hybrids that clearly show their *Clematis viticella* blood (see page 139). They have flowers 10–15cm (4–6in) across, produced from midsummer to early autumn, and are very resistant to wilt. They grow to around 3m (10ft) and are very free-flowering over a long period, making superb companions for roses.

Clematis 'Comtesse de Bouchaud'♥ is probably one of the best performers in this group, with richly textured, soft rose-pink flowers with cream anthers. It is a stunning plant and ideal for beginners.

Clematis 'Perle d'Azur', with its sky-blue flowers, is often cited as the best of all clematis, but it is certainly not the easiest. It tends to be a little gangly and will succumb to mildew at the slightest provocation. *Clematis* 'Prince Charles'♥ is a better plant, producing flowers in profusion; they are an unusual shade of light blue with a hint of mauve and washed with the merest hint of inky blue when they first open.

Another hybrid of similar colouring is *Clematis* 'Blekitny Aniol'♥, which has pale sky-blue flowers with wavy-edged

Clematis 'Comtesse de Bouchaud'

Clematis 'Perle d'Azur'

BURFORD HOUSE GARDENS

In the 1950s, clematis nurseryman and breeder John Treasure designed the 2.8-hectare (7-acre) gardens of this Georgian house beside the River Teme in Tenbury Wells, Worcestershire, establishing what is now a National Collection of texensis, viticella and herbaceous clematis. This comprises some 500 varieties, so summer visitors may well see as many as 80 in flower at once, often threading through other plants or along the ground.

sepals and greenish stamens. It is perhaps even overtaking *Clematis* 'Prince Charles' in popularity. *Clematis* 'Victoria'♔ has lovely, slightly squarer flowers with a mix of pink and blue in the sepals. This gives them a translucent appearance that is gorgeous mixed with roses.

Itea ilicifolia♔ is an unusual wall shrub, related to escallonia, that flowers in late summer. An evergreen with glossy, holly-like leaves, it has long, drooping, catkin-like racemes of honey-scented, greenish-white flowers. It likes a moist but well-drained soil and prefers a warm, sunny site, where it will reach 5m (16ft).

Most honeysuckles flower earlier in the season (see pages 128–129), but *Lonicera × heckrottii* 'Gold Flame' is one of the exceptions. It has fragrant yellow flowers, flushed with pink, at the ends of the new growth from midsummer through to early autumn. Its habit is somewhere between the climbing and shrubby honeysuckles and it grows to 5m (16ft).

Clematis 'Blekitny Aniol'

Itea ilicifolia

Lonicera × heckrottii 'Gold Flame'

LATE SUMMER

GOOD COMPANIONS

Campsis × tagliabuana 'Madame Galen'♔ (1) has a rich, exotic feel that sits well with Mediterranean plants, such as the steely blue palm, *Chamaerops humilis* var. *argentea* (2).

The strong purple flowers of *Clematis* 'Polish Spirit'♔ (3) contrast dramatically with the gorgeous orange of the tender perennial *Canna* TROPICANNA ('Phasion')♔ (4).

The blue-flowered *Rosmarinus officinalis* (5) thrives in a poor, well-drained soil and so is ideal planted in front of *Passiflora caerulea* 'White Lightning' (6).

137

CLEMATIS TEXENSIS

Clematis texensis is the aristocrat of the clematis family. It is often called the scarlet vine and is native to limestone areas with good, deep, moist soil, mainly between the Rio Grande and the Colorado River, where it scrambles among other plants. The true species can vary from scarlet to purple-red, but red-orange flowers with yellow throats are most sought after. The nodding flowers are tulip shaped, with sepals turned back at the tips, and the pinnate leaves are a matt, glaucous green.

Clematis texensis itself is not of great garden use: it is very variable from seed and difficult to propagate. The interest in it springs from its ability to bring the colour red into clematis breeding. We are so used to the idea of jewel-coloured clematis that we forget that in the mid-1900s the most dramatic colouring came from the viticella clematis (see opposite). This meant that there were blues and purples, but no reds. *Clematis texensis* changed all that.

As a group, texensis hybrids grow to around 3m (10ft). They tend to die off to ground level or nearly so in winter when the leaves have dropped. How far back they die determines when they start flowering the following year. With the right varieties in the right spot, you can have them in flower in early summer. Get it wrong and you will wait until late summer or even early autumn. Once in bloom, they continue to produce flowers on new growths until the frosts, making them very useful additions to the garden.

Although they will tolerate more extremes of soil than many other clematis, they will give their best only on a good, well-drained soil in a warm, sunny spot, needing sunshine to support their long flowering period. They are resistant to clematis wilt, but are susceptible to powdery mildew. If this is a problem in your garden, choose the varieties that are more resistant, or spray regularly with a fungicide.

For a true shade of pink, rare in the clematis world, choose **Clematis 'Duchess of Albany'** (1). Its candy-pink flowers fade to lilac-pink at the margins and have a darker pink central bar.

Clematis 'Gravetye Beauty' (2) has rich crimson flowers that open out fully to a star shape and make a stunning display. Not especially vigorous, this variety is best used trailing across low-growing shrubs. If the old wood survives the winter, the plant may flower in early summer; otherwise blooms will appear from late summer onwards.

Clematis 'Princess Diana' ♛ (3), also known as 'The Princess of Wales', is a very good plant. It is a vibrant shade of pink with a vivid pink central bar that fades to mauve-pink near the edges. A strong grower, it flowers for longer than most hybrids and is very resistant to mildew.

Clematis 'Sir Trevor Lawrence' (4) has flowers that are rich red on the inside and pale frosty pink outside. It blooms from midsummer to early autumn. Susceptible to mildew.

OTHER GOOD CLEMATIS TEXENSIS

Clematis 'Etoile Rose' Deep cherry purple with paler edges. It is sometimes considered more closely related to *Clematis viticella*, but from a cultural point of view it belongs here. Spray against mildew.

Clematis 'Lady Bird Johnson' A stunning, dark red-purple, in flower from late summer or early autumn onwards. Must be sprayed against powdery mildew.

CLEMATIS VITICELLA

A native of southern Europe, *Clematis viticella*♀ (the virgin's bower) has been cultivated in Britain since at least 1569, when the pharmacist to Queen Elizabeth I recorded growing it. It is a slender, deciduous climber with divided leaves and small, nodding, deep blue-purple flowers carried on long, elegant stalks from the young growth. While not the most dramatic of plants itself, it has been used to produce innumerable hybrids.

A very adaptable group, viticellas are capable of shimmying up roses, lighting up ground cover, clothing garden features and threading their way through shrubs (see pages 69 and 73). They are the easiest clematis, growing in most soils and in most positions, although they prefer a sunny spot. Pruning is easy (see page 33): simply cut back to 30cm (12in) in late winter. The plant will regrow and reach at least 3m (10ft) by late summer. Flowering starts in midsummer, perhaps earlier in sheltered gardens, and continues until mid-autumn. All viticellas are resistant to clematis wilt.

OTHER GOOD CLEMATIS VITICELLA

Clematis **'Betty Corning'**♀ Nodding, bell-shaped flowers with a light scent. Slightly shy to flower. Height 2m (6ft).

Clematis **'Blue Belle'** Large, deep violet-blue flowers.

Clematis **'Carmencita'** Nodding, deep carmine flowers with black anthers. Height 3.5m (12ft).

Clematis **'Kermesina'**♀ Crimson flowers with black anthers. Sepals have green tips early in the season.

Clematis **'Little Nell'** White flowers with pale pink margins and greenish-yellow anthers.

Clematis **'M. Koster'** Deep rose-pink flowers with greenish-yellow anthers and well-spaced sepals.

Clematis **'Royal Velours'**♀ Full flowers in lovely satin purple with greenish-black anthers. (See page 107.)

Clematis **'Södertalje'** Flowers are reddish pink with pale anthers.

Clematis **'Venosa Violacea'**♀ Highly distinctive white flowers attractively edged with purple.

Clematis **'Alba Luxurians'**♀ (**1**) has white sepals that turn back slightly at the tips and sometimes have a hint of blue along the middle. The flower tips often have a greenish tinge, but this usually wears off. The anthers are deepest aubergine.

Clematis **'Etoile Violette'**♀ (**2**) has an abundance of classic velvety, deep purple viticella flowers, with yellow anthers. Planted with red roses it is absolutely stunning.

Clematis **'Abundance'**♀ (**3**) freely produces soft rose-pink flowers with broad sepals and yellow anthers.

Clematis **'Madame Julia Correvon'**♀ (**4**) has rich red flowers with widely spaced sepals and yellow anthers. Good with grey foliage plants.

Clematis **'Polish Spirit'**♀ is a little more vigorous than some, happily taking on a larger shrub. It produces masses of rich green leaves, making it suitable to grow on its own up a pergola post. The flowers are a very strong purple with deep red anthers. (See Good Companions, page 137.)

Clematis **'Purpurea Plena Elegans'** is tough, hardy and easy to grow. The flowers have masses of red-flushed, violet-purple petal-like stamens arranged in rosette fashion, and often have green tips. Small, light foliage makes it ideal for growing through other plants. (See page 107.)

A SELECTION OF CLEMATIS THROUGH THE YEAR

Flowering time - Aspect - Flower size - Height - Pruning group (see page 33)

Early to mid-spring

Clematis armandii 'Enham Star' (see page 119)

Beautiful evergreen. Looks good clambering over large walls or up trees. Dislikes training.

Aspect Sunny

Flower size 4cm (2in)

Height 6m (20ft)

Pruning group 1

Early summer to early autumn

Clematis 'Allanah' (see page 105)

Free-flowering. Looks fantastic in pots.

Aspect Sunny

Flower size 12cm (5in)

Height 3m (10ft)

Pruning group 3

Mid- to late spring

Clematis 'Constance' ♔ (see page 120)

Good tempered, resilient. Superb in pots and on a garden feature.

Aspect Any

Flower size 5cm (2in)

Height 3m (10ft)

Pruning group 1

Early summer to early autumn

Clematis 'Alionushka' ♔ (see page 67)

Herbaceous habit, needs support. Perfect for growing through roses and shrubs.

Aspect Sunny

Flower size 6cm (3in)

Height 2m (6ft)

Pruning group 3

Late spring to early summer

Clematis macropetala 'Lagoon' ♔ (see page 122)

Very tough, cold-resistant. Silky seedheads. Great in pots or on arches.

Aspect Any

Flower size 6cm (3in)

Height 2.5m (8ft)

Pruning group 1

Midsummer to early autumn

Clematis 'Prince Charles' ♔ (see page 136)

Free-flowering. Can grow through small trees.

Aspect Sunny

Flower size 10cm (4in)

Height 3m (10ft)

Pruning group 3

Late spring to early summer

Clematis montana var. *rubens* 'Tetrarose' ♔ (see page 123)

Vigorous, quick-growing. Needs plenty of space. Lovely through trees.

Aspect Any

Flower size 7cm (3in)

Height 7.5m (25ft)

Pruning group 1

Midsummer to early autumn

Clematis 'Purpurea Plena Elegans' ♔ (see page 107)

Very reliable and long-flowering. Happy to grow through larger climbers.

Aspect Sunny

Flower size 7cm (3in)

Height 3.5m (12ft)

Pruning group 3

Late spring to early summer and late summer to early autumn

Clematis 'Fuji-musume' ♔ (see page 110)

Exceptionally free-flowering, compact, trouble-free. Good in pots.

Aspect Any

Flower size 12cm (5in)

Height 2.5m (8ft)

Pruning group 2

Midsummer to late autumn

Clematis 'Bill MacKenzie' ♔ (see page 48)

Vigorous and very free-flowering. Masses of silky seedheads mingle with the late flowers.

Aspect Sunny

Flower size 6cm (3in)

Height 6m (20ft)

Pruning group 3

Early to late summer and early autumn

Clematis 'Princess Diana' ♔ (see page 138)

Free-flowering, trouble-free. Best scrambling through shrubs.

Aspect Sunny

Flower size 6cm (3in)

Height 3m (10ft)

Pruning group 3

Mid- to late winter

Clematis cirrhosa var. *purpurascens* 'Freckles' ♔ (see page 150)

Ideal for evergreen screens and for all types of garden feature. Attractive foliage.

Aspect Sunny

Flower size 7cm (3in)

Height 4m (13ft)

Pruning group 1

Passion flower (Passiflora)

Climbing passion flowers (*Passiflora*) are usually vigorous evergreens, grown mainly for their intricate, bowl-shaped blooms, which missionaries used to illustrate the story of Christ's crucifixion. Virtually all are tropical or subtropical, needing the protection of a conservatory to survive in temperate climates; only *Passiflora caerulea*♀ and its forms are hardy enough to grow outside and even then only in a sheltered site. The hardier kinds all have flowers in shades of white or lavender and flower from summer to autumn. All have slender stems with deeply lobed leaves, and use twining tendrils to cling to their supports.

Soil is the key to success with passion flowers. In the wild, they grow on poor, very sandy, neutral or slightly alkaline soils in full sun. This is why they thrive on house walls where the builder's rubble usually left beneath the soil creates the perfect conditions. If overfed, they will produce masses of soft green growth but no flowers. A humus-rich, acid soil will cause them to fail, while very alkaline soil will cause severe yellowing of the leaves (chlorosis).

Passiflora × violacea has rich purple-red, fragrant flowers from summer through to autumn followed by green fruit. Height 5m (16ft) or more. Needs a conservatory in cold climates.

Allowing some stems to hang down from their support will encourage flowering: when the plant finds that its leading shoot cannot grow upwards, it begins to produce flower buds all along the length of the stem.

Passiflora caerulea♀ (blue passion flower) (**1**) is vigorous, reaching 10m (33ft) on a warm wall. It has scented, violet-blue and white flowers from early summer until the frosts. These are followed by bright orange fruit, which are edible but a bit disappointing.

Passiflora caerulea **'White Lightning'** (**2**) is a new introduction with masses of slightly fragrant, white flowers, with a blue tip to the stamens, and bright orange fruit. It blooms from late spring right through to the frosts. This is an exceptionally good, free-flowering cultivar, growing to 8m (26ft). Healthy and trouble-free, it looks an excellent alternative to *Passiflora caerulea* 'Constance Elliott', which for many years was the only white passion flower available but suffers badly from viral disease. The overall appearance of 'White

Lightning' is not as white as 'Constance Elliott', but its health and the sheer volume of flower more than compensate for this. (See Good Companions, page 137.)

Passiflora **'Amethyst'**♀ has scented, rich lavender-blue flowers from late summer through to autumn, followed by vivid orange fruit. Height 4m (13ft).

Passiflora **'Eden'** is a cross between *Passiflora caerulea* and *Passiflora* 'Amethyst', with large, lightly scented, soft lavender flowers edged with amethyst. These are freely produced from midsummer to the frosts and are followed by orange fruit. Grows to 6m (20ft). Good drainage is essential for it to succeed.

141

Autumn

Blazing shades of scarlet, flame, orange and gold dominate the autumn colour palette. Big bold leaves, berries and seedheads mingle to create a rich tapestry of texture and colour. This is a season where all plants are players, working as part of a much bigger picture rather than performing as individual stars.

Actinidia deliciosa 'Hayward'

For exotic looks, *Actinidia deliciosa* (kiwi fruit or Chinese gooseberry) is hard to beat. The stout stems and lush, heart-shaped leaves are covered in bristly, copper-coloured hairs, just like the ovoid, greenish-brown fruit that follows the white flowers. Deciduous, twining climbers, the plants are usually male or female; in a sheltered position the females, when pollinated by a male plant, will produce edible fruit in autumn. There are hermaphrodite forms, such as ***Actinidia deliciosa*** 'Jenny', with male and female flowers on the same plant, but the fruit is inferior. ***Actinidia deliciosa*** 'Hayward' is a good female form used commercially, while ***Actinidia deliciosa*** 'Tomuri' is a reliable male pollinator. Kiwis grow to 10m (33ft) and if you seriously wish to grow fruit you will need plenty of space to grow two plants. They need a rich, fertile soil, plenty of sun and shelter from damaging winds. Fruiting plants will need to be trained along wires and pruned back to a main framework in spring.

Closely related to *Vitis*, ***Ampelopsis brevipedunculata*** is a vigorous, luxuriant climber, clothed in lobed, dark green leaves that turn a pretty light yellow in autumn. It grows to 5m (16ft), climbing with the aid of twining stem tendrils, and

Planting autumn-colouring climbers such as *Vitis coignetiae* in full sun ensures the strongest autumn colour and allows the light to play on the leaves, highlighting their form and colour.

THE CHANGE TO AUTUMN COLOUR

The autumn leaf colour of deciduous climbers and wall shrubs such as *Parthenocissus*, *Wisteria*, *Hydrangea* and *Vitis* (*Vitis* 'Brant'♀, below; see also page 145), gives us some of the most breathtaking sights of the year. But what is it that causes the leaves to change colour?

In autumn, the fall in light levels and temperature triggers changes in plants that reduce the flow of nutrients to the leaves. This halts the production of new chlorophyll, the pigment that gives leaves their green colour. Low temperatures also break down any existing green pigment, and so the other pigments present in the leaf are unmasked. The principal ones are carotene, which makes leaves appear yellow, and anthocyanin, which gives the purplish-red shades.

Temperatures above freezing promote the production of anthocyanins, as does sunshine. If the weather is wet, anthocyanin production is slowed. Hence dry, sunny days and cool, dry nights bring the most spectacular autumn colour.

Ampelopsis brevipedunculata

Clematis tangutica

Clematis tibetana subsp. *vernayi*

produces insignificant green flowers in summer. In autumn, in a sunny position and after a hot summer, it produces small, verdigris to deep blue fruit. *Ampelopsis brevipedunculata* var. *maximowiczii* 'Elegans' (see page 39) has richly variegated leaves but is weak-growing.

Ampelopsis aconitifolia 'Chinese Lace' has superb autumn colour, the very finely cut leaves turning from orange and yellow to red as the season progresses. It is a vigorous grower, reaching a height of 10m (33ft).

Clematis tibetana subsp. *vernayi* (formerly *Clematis orientalis*) bears its nodding, yellow flowers from midsummer until the autumn frosts. Silky seedheads are carried at the same time to great effect. The sepals are thick, like orange peel, and bend back beyond the horizontal when the flowers are fully open. This is a deciduous climber and grows to 7m (22ft). Two other yellow clematis that

are particularly good for their autumn seedheads, which last well into winter, are *Clematis tangutica* and *Clematis* 'Bill MacKenzie'♀ (see page 48 and Good Companions, page 145).

Clematis 'Golden Harvest' is a darker-flowered variety of *Clematis serratifolia*. It carries a really good crop of rich yellow, nodding, four-sepalled flowers with dark purple stamens from summer through to autumn, followed by masses of silky seedheads. It grows to 4m (13ft) and has divided, deciduous foliage of an attractive bright green.

Clematis 'Madame Baron-Veillard' probably flowers later than any other clematis hybrid. It starts producing its pale lilac-pink flowers with green anthers only in early autumn but continues until the frosts. It needs a sunny spot and is very vigorous, growing to 4m (13ft). This is a good hybrid for the USA, where it has proved very hardy.

PYRACANTHA

Pyracanthas were once classified as *Cotoneaster* but their thorny stems led to them getting their new name. *Pyracantha* is taken from the Greek: *pyr* meaning fire and *akanthos* meaning a thorn, referring to the blazing colours of the berries and to the thorny branches. They are evergreens that can be grown as free-standing shrubs or dense hedges, but are more usually seen as wall shrubs. They take well to both formal and informal use, looking just as much at home spilling across a cottage wall as being trained to form perfect geometric shapes on the walls of stately homes.

The creamy-white, hawthorn-like flowers are carried in clusters all along the stems. The glossy green, ovate leaves set off the bunches of yellow, orange or red berries that appear on the branches in autumn. The branches should be treated with caution as the spines can be extremely sharp.

Pyracanthas will grow in almost any soil but unless it is warm, deep and well-drained they may be more susceptible to scab, a disfiguring bacterial disease that causes the fruit to split and creates dark patches on the leaves. A sunny or partly shaded site is best for flowers and fruit. Although there are several species, it is the hybrids that have made their way into our gardens.

Pyracantha 'Soleil d'Or' (**1**) grows to 3.5m (12ft), with upright branches and reddish stems. The leaves are dark, glossy green and the berries are golden yellow.

Pyracantha 'Mohave' (**2**) has early-ripening, long-lasting red berries. It is beautiful but very prone to scab. Grows to 5m (16ft).

Pyracantha coccinea 'Red Column' (**3**) is upright, growing to 4m (13ft) against a wall, with early-ripening clusters of dense red berries, much loved by blackbirds. The shoots are reddish in colour and the glossy green leaves are sharply toothed.

Pyracantha 'Orange Glow'♟ (**4**) is a very hardy plant that carries masses of tightly packed, orange-red berries that colour in early autumn and last well through the winter. It is ideal for a wall, where it will reach 4m (13ft). (See Good Companions, right.)

OTHER GOOD PYRACANTHAS

Pyracantha 'Golden Charmer'♟
Has a somewhat misleading name as the berries are more orange than yellow. Bears masses of fruit but needs a large wall. Scab resistant. 4m (13ft).

Pyracantha rogersiana 'Flava'♟
Free-fruiting, tall variety, reaching 5m (16ft), with small leaves and golden yellow fruit.

Pyracantha 'Teton'♟ Large and upright plant, growing to 6m (20ft), with small, orange-yellow fruit.

Vitis 'Brant'

Schisandra rubriflora is a somewhat shy-flowering, twining climber growing to 10m (33ft) and with deep red flowers in late spring and summer, among lance-shaped leaves that turn golden yellow in autumn before falling. Female plants produce showy, pendent spikes, 15cm (6in) long, of scarlet berries, which remain on the plant. Grow it in sun or partial shade and in soil with plenty of added organic matter.

If you are planning to provide shade for a seating area, consider the fruiting vine, *Vitis vinifera*. A very sunny position is needed if it is to produce fruit. These fast-growing, deciduous, stem-tendril climbers have been grown since ancient times for both the fruit produced from late summer and the brilliant autumn leaf colours. They thrive best on well-drained, fertile, neutral to alkaline, humus-rich soil.

There are many varieties that will grow outside and give high-quality grapes, including **Vitis vinifera 'Chardonnay'**,

Schisandra rubriflora

Vitis vinifera

GOOD COMPANIONS

Clematis 'Bill MacKenzie'♥ (1) makes a stunning autumn composition when planted with the vibrant orange flowers of *Crocosmia* × *crocosmiiflora* 'Emily McKenzie' (2) at its base.

Hydrangea quercifolia 'Little Honey' (3) has large, bold, buttery-yellow autumn leaves on a compact plant. It is superb tucked at the foot of *Pyracantha* 'Orange Glow'♥ (4), the leaves contrasting with the berries.

Thread the red *Clematis* 'Madame Julia Correvon'♥ (5) through *Parthenocissus tricuspidata* 'Veitchii' (6), and the red flowers borne from midsummer will give a taste of the foliage colour to come later in the season.

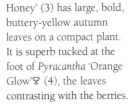

Vitis 'Phönix' and *Vitis vinifera* 'Pinot Noir'. The Great Vine at Hampton Court Palace in London, planted in 1768 by Capability Brown, is the oldest grape vine in the world and it is now possible to buy a cutting from this famous plant. The cultivar is *Vitis vinifera* 'Schiava Grossa' (BLACK HAMBURGH); given a hot, sunny wall and well-drained soil, it will grow as large as your pruning allows.

Vitis 'Brant'♥ is another popular hardy fruiting vine, carrying bunches of dark purple-black, bloomy grapes. The big, bold, five-lobed leaves turn dramatic shades of dark red and purple with green veins in autumn. It needs plenty of space, since it grows quickly to 9m (30ft).

Vitis coignetiae♥ is a wonderful autumn vine. Larger than *Vitis* 'Brant', it grows to 15m (50ft) and has more heart-shaped leaves. They turn rich red in autumn in the sun; leaves in the lower layer stay yellow, giving an amazing depth to the plant. (See pages 71 and 142.)

Parthenocissus

Parthenocissus are mostly deciduous, self-clinging climbers much prized for their autumn foliage colour. Unfortunately the common name Virginia creeper is used for many of its species, so if you go to a nursery or garden centre and simply ask for a Virginia creeper, you may not get the plant you want. The true Virginia creeper is *Parthenocissus quinquefolia*♔, discovered during the days of the Pilgrim Fathers in the state of Virginia, USA. *Parthenocissus tricuspidata*♔ has also been given the name but it is in fact a plant from China and Japan and should be called either Japanese creeper or Boston ivy.

Both are extremely good grown against a wall, but are also striking when allowed to run up the trunk of a tree. A flame-red parthenocissus growing against the white bark of a birch (*Betula*) is a stunning sight. All parthenocissus love well-drained, fertile soil and grow in sun or shade, usually producing a small crop of blue-black berries in late summer.

When you plant parthenocissus, make sure that the stems are held securely against the wall or fence with canes or lead-headed nails. This enables the tendrils to fix their pads firmly to the surface. Once they have a foothold, the stems tend to grow vertically, so it is a good idea to spread the young stems out horizontally to cover a wider area.

Parthenocissus tricuspidata♔ (Boston ivy or Japanese creeper) has pretty, three-lobed leaves of clear green. In autumn they turn glorious shades of red and purple, with odd flashes of gold where the leaves are shaded from the sun. It grows to a huge 20m (65ft), making it an ideal choice for really big walls. There are several selected varieties, each with its own charm.

When mature, parthenocissus can prove too heavy a weight for their tendrils to support. An annual or biennial trim in spring, cutting back some of the oldest stems, will help keep plenty of young growth forming to hold on to the wall and will also reduce the overall weight of the plant.

Parthenocissus himalayana var. *rubrifolia* is a strong-growing climber, reaching 10m (33ft), with large leaves that are purple when young, turning rich crimson in autumn. It is rather tender but is the best representative of this species for gardens.

OTHER GOOD PARTHENOCISSUS

Parthenocissus tricuspidata **'Beverley Brook'** More compact than the species, growing to 3m (10ft), and has fairly small, bright green leaves that are bronze when young and turn deep red in autumn.

Parthenocissus tricuspidata **'Green Spring'** Very vigorous with large, bright green leaves up to 25cm (10in), bronze when young and red-purple in autumn. Grows to 8m (26ft).

Parthenocissus tricuspidata **'Lowii'** Small, lobed foliage, giving a cut-leaved appearance. Colours to rich mahogany in autumn. Very slow-growing, reaching only 3m (10ft).

Parthenocissus quinquefolia♀ (Virginia creeper) (**1**) has five-lobed, toothed leaves in a soft mid-green. In autumn the foliage turns a wonderful fiery red. It reaches 15m (50ft). This species had become scarce, being replaced with *Parthenocissus tricuspidata*, but it was reintroduced in the early 20th century and is now once again quite widely spread.

Parthenocissus tricuspidata **'Veitchii'** (**2**) has smaller leaves than the species, purple when young turning to a dark plum in autumn. It grows to 8m (26ft).

Parthenocissus henryana♀ (**3**) produces attractive, silver-veined, green leaves that sometimes have a pink flush. In autumn the leaves turn a really good red with lighter veins. It reaches 10m (33ft).

Winter

Glittering, brittle and crisp: winter has a light unlike any other time of the year. Whether grey, misty and brooding or brilliantly sunny and freezing cold, winter days have a special atmosphere. Flowers are scarce so each one is all the more precious. Evergreens take on a new importance, providing vegetable masonry, their stark strong lines complementing subtle palettes of flower colour.

Choosing climbers and wall shrubs for winter colour demands particular care because they have not only to fulfil their winter brief but also to fit into the garden in the rest of the year, when they may not necessarily have much to offer. Take a good look at the foliage of any climber or shrub you consider: if good, the plant can contribute interest all year round; if not,

it can be disguised by planting another climber, perhaps a flowering one, through it. Threading a variegated plant such as *Hedera helix* 'Goldheart' (officially *Hedera helix* 'Oro di Bogliasco', see page 101) or *Solanum laxum* 'Album Variegatum' (see page 41) through a winter-flowering climber can really pack a seasonal punch. Planting winter flowers such as hellebores

Flowers seem particularly valuable in cold winter weather. In mild years camellias like this *williamsii* hybrid 'Saint Ewe' will produce early flowers even as the garden is still firmly in the grip of winter.

and snowdrops at their base also adds to the effect. Some climbers and wall shrubs with winter flowers have a lovely fragrance and you might want to plant these close to a door or window, where

Abeliophyllum distichum

Camellia × vernalis 'Yuletide'

Camellia sasanqua 'Kenkyo'

Camellia sasanqua 'Crimson King'

they can be enjoyed from the warmth of the house, or where you will pass them when you enter or leave.

Think carefully about backgrounds in winter when there is little foliage around. The deciduous wall shrub *Abeliophyllum distichum* (see page 38) gives white, fragrant flowers on bare branches in late winter, but these will be lost if the plant is set against a light-coloured wall.

Evergreens have a natural advantage in winter time and *Camellia sasanqua* is an evergreen shrub with class. It is not brash and vulgar with huge flowers; instead it has small, elegant, scented, white flowers, a few appearing in late autumn with the main crop through the winter. The leaves are a lovely glossy green, dark above, lighter below. It tends to be a lax, long-limbed plant and is best trained against a wall, where it will grow to 6m (20ft).

Camellia sasanqua stands more sun than *Camellia japonica* (see page 117). In Britain it will grow outside on a wall in the south, but needs a conservatory further north. It also grows especially well in California. The flowers sometimes get damaged in frosts, but new ones will replace them. This plant can be difficult when young, developing spotty leaves, but these grow through with time, and the species gets hardier as it matures.

There are many hybrids but *Camellia sasanqua* 'Narumigata', with creamy-white, pink-edged flowers, is probably the hardiest and most reliable. Other hybrids worth hunting out are the red 'Crimson King'⚱ and the white 'Kenkyo'. *Camellia × vernalis* 'Yuletide', a cross between *Camellia sasanqua* and *Camellia japonica*, is a superb red hybrid, flowering from late winter through to mid-spring.

Camellia sasanqua 'Narumigata'

149

CLEMATIS CIRRHOSA

A native of places with warm climates all around the Mediterranean Sea, *Clematis cirrhosa* can be grown successfully outside in many parts of Britain. From mid- to late winter, it has small, nodding, bell-shaped, cream flowers, sometimes with red spots, borne among dainty, much divided leaves of glossy, dark green, and followed by attractive silky seedheads.

It is evergreen but, like *Clematis napaulensis* (see page 151), it becomes dormant in summer. Growth restarts in autumn when the temperature cools and rain falls more often. It is a scrambler, growing to 4m (13ft), and prefers to keep its roots cool and its flowers in the sun. It likes a well-drained, fertile soil.

Clematis cirrhosa var. *balearica* (**1**) is a long-established variety, originally found on Minorca in 1783, with lemon-scented, pale yellow bells, spotted with plum. It is smaller-growing than the species, reaching 3m (10ft), and flowers from late autumn through to early spring. The foliage is finely cut, giving the plant the common name of fern-leaved clematis, and turns bronze in winter. It is not as hardy as the species.

Clematis cirrhosa var. *purpurascens* is a newly created group that encompasses the varieties with speckled flowers found on Mallorca and Gibraltar and in northern Algeria. They have become known as the hellebore clematis and are proving the most popular forms in gardens.

Clematis cirrhosa var. *purpurascens* 'Freckles'♔ (**2**) is the most widely available hellebore clematis. It has masses of plum spots all over the cream flowers, even spreading to the outside.

Clematis cirrhosa var. *purpurascens* 'Jingle Bells' (**3**) is a selection made from 'Freckles' with nodding, creamy-white or yellow flowers with pale yellow anthers. It is paler than 'Wisley Cream'♔ and said to be hardier and more free-flowering.

Clematis cirrhosa 'Wisley Cream'♔ (**4**) was the first named spotless form, raised from seed collected in southern Europe. It has creamy-green flowers, produced from late autumn to early spring.

PRUNING CLEMATIS CIRRHOSA

It is very tempting to trim this clematis in the autumn but every cut will remove flower buds. The plant needs pruning only if it has outgrown its space. Prune lightly immediately after flowering in early spring to allow new growth to form and set buds for the winter.

If you miss the correct pruning time, simply bend the offending stems gently round and redirect them back into the area to be covered. If need be, you can cut them out next year.

OTHER GOOD CLEMATIS CIRRHOSA

Clematis cirrhosa 'Ourika Valley' A little-known variety with clear yellow-cream flowers and attractive cut foliage.

Clematis cirrhosa var. *purpurascens* 'Lansdowne Gem' In this variety, the spots have melted together to form a solid colour – a glorious shade of dull claret with a silver-grey reverse.

Clematis cirrhosa var. *purpurascens* 'Stargazer' A new form with recurved flowers like those of 'Jingle Bells'.

Clematis cirrhosa subsp. *semitriloba* Very similar to *Clematis cirrhosa* var. *balearica* and often mistaken for it, but the flowers have stripes of plum at the centre.

Clematis napaulensis is a very unusual winter-flowering, tender climber, well worth considering for a sheltered wall or a conservatory. It is deciduous and grows to 4m (13ft). The flowers are long, cup shaped and creamy yellow, with extra-long purple stamens, and are followed in spring by fluffy seedheads. The foliage persists through the winter, and the plant becomes dormant in late summer, growing again in late autumn.

The deliciously scented, evergreen *Daphne bholua* 'Jacqueline Postill'♛ is usually grown as a free-standing shrub, but in colder areas it benefits from the protection of a warm wall. The white flowers are tinted pink and are produced in small clusters from midwinter to early spring. The growth is upright, to 3.5m (12ft), and ideal for a narrow wall space. It loves a sunny position with well-drained soil. (See Good Companions, below.)

A classic choice for winter is the silk tassel bush, *Garrya elliptica.* This bold,

Clematis napaulensis

Daphne bholua 'Jacqueline Postill'

Garrya elliptica 'James Roof'

Jasminum nudiflorum

evergreen shrub has grey-green, slightly wrinkled, leathery leaves and, in late winter and early spring, produces long, greenish-grey catkins. The cultivar **'James Roof'**♛ has especially long catkins, which hang dramatically from the branches. It likes well-drained soil and a sheltered position; against a wall it grows to 4m (13ft). (See Good Companions, left.)

The winter jasmine, *Jasminum nudiflorum*♛, is easy to grow, even in poor soil. Up to 4.5m (15ft) high, it makes an excellent wall shrub or informal hedge and produces its bright yellow (though unscented) flowers on bare stems from late autumn to early spring. This is a familiar plant but it should not be underrated for it provides a cheering sight in winter. (See Good Companions, left.)

GOOD COMPANIONS

The jewel-like colours of *Helleborus hybridus* Hillier hybrids (1) look fantastic crowded at the feet of *Garrya elliptica* 'James Roof'♛ (2), with its grey-green, evergreen foliage and elegant silver tassels.

Narcissus 'Martinette' (3) echoes the colour of winter jasmine, *Jasminum nudiflorum*♛ (4), and provides the fragrance that the jasmine lacks.

The deep plum, evergreen foliage of *Pittosporum tenuifolium* 'Tom Thumb'♛ (5) complements the dark pink flush in the flowers of *Daphne bholua* 'Jacqueline Postill'♛ (6).

151

PLANT PROFILE

Ivy (Hedera)

Ivies tend to be regarded as too commonplace for use in today's gardens, yet they are among the most successful climbers we grow. Evergreen, self-clinging climbers or trailers, they can be used in innumerable ways: for ground cover, low and high walls, topiary, slim screens and growing through trees. They make excellent backdrops to other climbers, and on the ground they look lovely underplanted with bulbs between other low-growing plants. Many hundreds of varieties are available, varying enormously in both size and vigour, and with foliage in every shade from bright butter yellow to rich green, cool grey and dark plum. Leaf size ranges from dainty and small to huge and bold, and leaf shape varies incredibly, from simple heart shapes to claw-like talons. The English ivy, *Hedera helix*, seems to mutate very freely and the majority of cultivars are within this species. (See also pages 48, 52, 69, 72–73, 76, 97, 101 and 113.)

Ivies have two very distinct stages of growth. At the juvenile, climbing stage they produce long, straight stems with strong aerial roots that enable them to fix firmly to their supports. The adult stage is when the flowers appear. At this point, the growth becomes bushy and grows away from its supports. The greenish-yellow autumn flowers develop into airy branches covered with rounded heads of matt black berries, much prized by flower arrangers. The fruit make useful food for birds and the branched growth provides valuable nesting cover. The leafy foliage is also a safe haven for a large number of insects.

Some ivies are extremely hardy plants, surviving the worst of winter weather completely unscathed, but others are more tender, and in colder climates suitable only for growing as houseplants or in a conservatory, or for use as summer bedding plants.

Ivy will grow in almost any soil but fares best in alkaline conditions, with reasonable moisture at the roots. It does not seem to mind whether it is in sun

Hedera helix 'Atropurpurea' The leaves of this variety are quite dark green in summer, taking on a purplish colour in winter except for the veins, which stay a contrasting green. It is hardy and vigorous, reaching 8m (26ft).

or shade and does well in both, but given the choice it will always grow from a shady position towards the light, whether by crossing open ground, growing across walls or scaling trees. No regular pruning is needed; simply trim the stems as necessary to keep the plant within its allotted space.

Hedera helix 'Buttercup' is a stunning plant, lovely on a low wall, with leaves of a rich buttery yellow. It is perfectly happy in shade and grows to 2m (6ft). Very hardy. (See also page 101.)

Hedera helix (English ivy) (**1**) is a very adaptable woodland plant, thriving in all soils and situations, even in dry shade. It is extremely hardy and very easy to grow, with glossy green, three-lobed leaves. It will easily reach 10m (33ft), but because it is variable from seed it can produce smaller offspring. (See also pages 52 and 73.)

Hedera helix 'Clotted Cream' (**2**) has soft, creamy-margined green leaves with lightly ruffled edges and grows to 8m (26ft). It is not a very stable sport, and the degree of ruffling on the leaf edges can vary. At its best it is lovely.

Hedera helix 'Très Coupé' (**3**) has deeply cut, three-lobed, dark green leaves. Suitable for ground cover or low walls, reaching 1m (40in). Hardy.

Hedera helix 'Golden Curl' (**4**) has bold, green and yellow splashed leaves, with curled edges. Prone to revert to plain green. Hardy. Grows to 2m (6ft).

Hedera canariensis (Canary ivy) should more correctly be called *Hedera algeriensis* but the name has become so firmly entrenched in common use that it has been decided to leave well alone. It has large, green leaves that bronze in winter and it grows to 4m (13ft). It needs a sheltered spot to succeed.

Hedera canariensis 'Gloire de Marengo'♥ is the most popular variety of the Canary ivy, with deep green leaves touched at the edges with silver and cream. It must have a warm wall otherwise it will be disappointing, losing foliage in winter. Height 3m (10ft).

Hedera canariensis 'Marginomaculata'♥ (**5**) has beautiful spotted leaves of all shades of green, cream and white. A tender ivy, often suffering winter damage. Grows to 4m (13ft).

Hedera colchica♥ (Persian ivy) is a handsome, strong-growing climber. It has dark green, leathery leaves, the largest of all ivy species, with a resinous aroma when crushed. It is taller than *Hedera canariensis*, reaching 10m (33ft), but grows more slowly and is much hardier.

Hedera colchica 'Dentata Variegata'♥ (**6**), the first hardy variegated ivy, is superb, with light green leaves mottled with grey and edged creamy white. A strong grower, it reaches a height of 5m (16ft). (See also page 69.)

Hedera colchica 'Dentata'♥ is very hardy, with large, soft green leaves. Grows to 10m (33ft).

MORE GOOD IVIES

Hedera colchica 'Sulphur Heart'♥ An exceptional plant, very hardy, with dark green leaves splashed with yellow and pale green. Grows to 10m (33ft). (See pages 69 and 101.)

Hedera helix 'Glymii' Similar to *Hedera helix* 'Atropurpurea' but with twisted leaves. Height 2m (6ft).

Hedera helix 'Königer's Auslese' Very hardy, with claw-like, five-lobed, mid-green leaves. Grows to 4m (13ft).

Author's choice:
favourite climbers and wall shrubs

Throughout the book I have described climbers and wall shrubs for many different uses. Here, I have grouped some of the very best. These are all tried and tested varieties that will do well for you. Within each group the plants share some characteristics while having different qualities – some have attractive foliage, others lovely flowers, and many have both – but all are top-performing climbers or wall shrubs.

QUICK-GROWING

Clematis montana var. *rubens* 'Tetrarose'♛ (page 123) Masses of dark rosy-mauve flowers late spring to early summer; bronze foliage. Vigorous and tough.

Humulus lupulus 'Aureus'♛ (page 102) Boisterous herbaceous, golden-leaved climber with swags of hops in autumn on female plants.

Parthenocissus tricuspidata♛ (page 146) Self-clinging, foliage climber; green in summer with stunning red and purple autumn colour.

Vitis coignetiae♛ (page 145) Bold, architectural foliage climber, brilliant autumn colour.

Wisteria sinensis 'Amethyst' (page 125) Free-flowering climber with highly scented, rich violet-blue flowers in spring; deep bronze young foliage.

SELF-CLINGING

Campsis × *tagliabuana* 'Madame Galen'♛ (page 39) Exotic-looking climber with salmon-red flowers late summer to early autumn; long, arching stems.

Euonymus fortunei 'Silver Queen' (page 88) Evergreen climber with grey-green leaves edged with creamy white; compact and reliable.

Hedera colchica 'Sulphur Heart'♛ (page 101) Extremely hardy, evergreen climber with big, bold leaves splashed with yellow and pale green.

Hydrangea anomala subsp. *petiolaris*♛ (page 44) Hardy climber with deep green leaves and pretty, white, lacecap-type flowers in summer.

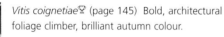
Parthenocissus quinquefolia♛ (page 147) Handsome foliage climber with large, five-lobed leaves, green in summer then fiery red in autumn.

ANNUAL

Cobaea scandens♛ (page 75) Bell-shaped, old rose-purple flowers from midsummer, followed by egg-shaped fruit in autumn.

Ipomoea tricolor 'Heavenly Blue' (page 112) Sensational azure, funnel-shaped flowers lasting for only a day but freely produced all summer.

Lathyrus odoratus 'Matucana' (page 75) Richly scented sweet pea with two-tone, maroon-purple and purple-blue flowers in summer.

Thunbergia alata (page 81) Large, yellow or orange flowers with a bold chocolate-purple eye, from summer through to autumn.

Tropaeolum majus (page 81) Edible, peppery-flavoured, orange, red or yellow flowers all summer and autumn.

FREE-FLOWERING

Clematis 'Fuji-musume'♛ (page 110) Exceptional clematis with stunning sky-blue flowers produced over a long period.

Jasminum nudiflorum♛ (page 99) Twiggy wall shrub with brilliant yellow flowers from late autumn to early spring.

Lonicera japonica 'Halliana'♛ (page 53) Semi-evergreen climber with scented, creamy-white and honey-yellow flowers all summer and into autumn.

Passiflora caerulea 'White Lightning' (page 141) Evergreen climber freely producing white flowers from late spring until frosts.

Rosa 'Madame Alfred Carrière'♛ (page 130) Very free-flowering climbing rose with sweetly scented, white blooms all through summer.

FOR NARROW SPACES

Ampelopsis brevipedunculata var. *maximowiczii* 'Elegans' (page 39) Slender climber with leaves splashed with pink and white.

Clematis 'Hagley Hybrid' (page 47) Reliable clematis with dusky mauve-pink flowers from early summer to early autumn.

Hedera helix 'Buttercup' (page 101) Evergreen self-clinger with buttery gold leaves, fading very slowly to green, and golden berries.

Jasminum officinale FIONA SUNRISE ('Frojas') (page 103) Twining climber with rich yellow foliage and a scattering of white, scented flowers in summer.

Rosa WARM WELCOME ('Chewizz')♀ (page 132) Miniature climbing rose with brilliant orange-red flowers very freely produced in summer.

Trachelospermum asiaticum 'Golden Memories' (page 103) Evergreen, small-leaved twiner with richly scented, creamy-white flowers in summer.

FOR NEW GARDENS

Abutilon × *suntense* 'Jermyns'♀ (page 38) Evergreen wall shrub smothered in clear mauve flowers from late spring to midsummer.

Ceanothus impressus (page 87) Bushy, small-leaved, evergreen wall shrub with clear blue flowers from mid- to late spring.

Clematis 'Comtesse de Bouchaud'♀ (page 136) Easy climber covered in rose-pink flowers from mid-summer to early autumn.

Fremontodendron 'California Glory'♀ (page 89) Unusual evergreen wall shrub carrying rich, egg-yellow flowers all through summer.

Rosa CONSTANCE SPRY ('Ausfirst')♀ (page 65) Climbing rose with big, old-fashioned style, cupped, clear pink, fragrant blooms in summer.

Solanum crispum 'Glasnevin'♀ (page 40) Very floriferous scrambler with bright purple flowers all summer and into autumn; semi-evergreen.

EVERGREEN

Camellia × *williamsii* 'Donation'♀ (page 42) Lovely wall shrub – the very best camellia; masses of semi-double, pale pink flowers from mid- to late spring.

Clematis cirrhosa var. *purpurascens* 'Freckles'♀ (page 150) Winter-flowering clematis with bell-shaped, creamy-white flowers covered in plum spots.

Garrya elliptica 'James Roof'♀ (page 151) Classic wall shrub with leathery, grey-green leaves and long, greenish-grey catkins in late winter and early spring.

Hedera helix 'Oro di Bogliasco' (known as 'Goldheart') (page 101) Distinctive ivy with small, deep green leaves with a gold centre; pinkish stems.

Magnolia grandiflora 'Goliath' (page 40) Large wall shrub, with huge, intensely fragrant, creamy flowers midsummer to mid-autumn; bold evergreen foliage.

Sophora SUN KING ('Hilsop')♀ (page 100) Wall shrub with clusters of bell-like, rich yellow flowers in late winter and early spring.

SCENTED

Daphne bholua 'Jacqueline Postill'♀ (page 151) Superb evergreen wall shrub with clusters of pink-tinted white flowers from midwinter to early spring.

Lonicera periclymenum 'Sweet Sue' (page 129) Compact climber with creamy-yellow flowers from early to late summer.

Jasminum officinale♀ (page 127) Semi-evergreen climber with starry, white flowers from early summer to early autumn; deep green foliage.

Rosa GERTRUDE JEKYLL ('Ausbord')♀ (page 65) Exceptionally healthy rose with flat, rich pink flowers all summer long.

Stephanotis floribunda♀ (page 61) Tender, evergreen climber with waxy, star-shaped flowers from spring to autumn.

Trachelospermum jasminoides♀ (page 96) Climber with glossy, evergreen foliage and showers of white, starry flowers all summer long.

Index

AUTHOR'S ACKNOWLEDGMENTS
Thanks to Leslie and Janet Dale for giving a green student the best possible start in the business, and to Andrew McIndoe for indulging my passion for climbers with this book. Most importantly, much love to my long-suffering husband, David, and daughters, Alexandra and Eloise.

PICTURE CREDITS
The publishers would like to acknowledge with thanks all those whose gardens are pictured in this book.

All photography by Philippa Bensley, Andrew McIndoe and John Hillier except: Burall Floraprint 89c; Kevin Hobbs 76a, 83d, 145 Good Companions (2), 149a,

150a, 151 Good Companions (1); Terry Underhill 54b, 71b.

Thanks are due to the following for the use of additional images:
New Leaf Plants (clematis and other climbers), David Austin Roses (roses) and Duncan and Davies (camellias).